U.S.S. Constitution

Postal Covers 1931 - 1934

By Paul St Pierre
2024 - Edition 4

Officers of the U. S. Frigate *Constitution* during
the East/West Cruise
(From left to right: Lieutenant David W. Tolson, Lieutenant W. J. Dean,
Lieutenant Commander Henry Hartley (executive officer), Commander Louis
J. Gulliver (captain), Lieutenant Joseph C. Van Cleve, Lieutenant J. Y.
Dannenberg and Lieutenant D. W. Lyon)

Preface

The Hon. John F. Fitzgerald, a former mayor of Boston and a Congressman in Washington, presented a bill which resulted in saving the *Constitution* and bringing her back to the Charleston Navy Yard. But for him and his patriotic sentiment toward "Old Ironsides", she would have had her fittings sold for junk and her hull towed out to sea and used as a target by our more modern ships.

For many years she lay at Charleston Navy Yard, slowly rotting away, waiting for plans and additional funds to restore her to her former prime condition. Then, in 1924, Admiral Edward Walter Eberle, Chief of Naval Operations, ordered the Board of Inspection and Survey to compile a report on the condition of the *Constitution*. The inspection of February 1924 found her in grave condition. Water had to be pumped out of her hold every day just to keep her afloat, and her stern was in danger of falling off. Almost all deck areas and structural components were filled with rot, and she was considered to be on the verge of ruin. Yet the Board recommended that she be thoroughly repaired in order to preserve her as long as possible. The estimated cost of repairs at that time was $400,000. Secretary of the Navy Curtis D. Wilbur proposed to Congress that the required funds be raised privately. The Secretary, however, took the attitude that "it would be a fine gesture on the part of the people of the country, and particularly the school children, if they contributed small donations for the purpose." He was authorized to assemble the committee charged with her restoration. Wilbur formally appointed Admiral Louis de Steiger to lead the National Save Old Ironsides campaign committee.

As envisioned by the Secretary of the Navy, the committee's initial fundraising ideas were to "popularize the campaign among the school children of the country and obtain from them in small sums the amount necessary," and gain larger contributions from patriotic societies and organizations based on Secretary Wilbur's general plan. The plan raised substantial funds and restoration began. Lieutenant John A. Lord was selected to oversee the reconstruction project, and work began while fund-raising efforts were still underway. Restoration was completed in 1930. Meanwhile, Charles Francis Adams had been appointed as Secretary of the Navy, and he proposed that *Constitution* make a tour of the United States upon her completion, as a gift to the nation for its efforts to help restore her. On July 1, 1931, Adm. Louis M. Nulton presided over the commission ceremonies and gave command of the *Constitution* to Cmdr. Louis J. Gulliver. The very next day, July 2, 1931, Constitution embarked on her 90 port East/West Cruise.

It was decided that cachet envelopes would be made available to visitors as mementos or souvenirs. This book is to show the various envelopes which were made available. The book is in three sections. First being 'Ship Cachets' which were applied by the mail clerk to envelopes which did not have an official or unofficial cachet. Second, "Envelope Cachets' are cachets placed on covers by individuals and/or organizations for use at any port or date. Third, 'Official Cachets' were offered by individuals and/or organizations free to all who sent covers and 'Private Cachets' which were applied by individuals and clubs for personal use, sale, or profit.

Covers listed here are to give the reader a reference for those covers which were available. This work is not intended to serve as a catalog of cachets but rather a reference for those available. Since the 'Ship Cachets' and 'Envelope Cachets' were available at any port on any date, they are listed here first and are not listed for each port. Official and Private cachets are listed once for each port. As many cachets were available in multiple colors, only one image is shown for reference. Images for the cachets listed within were pictured as in "The 1931-1934 Cruise of the U.S. Frigate *Constitution*" by Clarence L. Gwynne and by my personal cover collection. The reader must bear in mind that there may be other cachets available which are not listed here. Also, a grateful acknowledgment must be given to Skip Eckel for his contribution to this work. Although this book contains some info on the cruise itself, the main purpose is to highlight the many thousands of postal covers produced.

In researching for this book, I found this item by Charles L. Albright in his 1934 book "The East Coast Cruise of the U.S. Frigate *Constitution*" to be of interest. He includes the following:

"There has been considerable argument on the correct title of the Frigate *Constitution*. Some state that the ship is called the *U. S. S. Constitution* while others claim that the correct title is U. S. Frigate *Constitution*. To settle the argument, and to correct the erroneous impression of some secretaries of Chambers of Commerce and others, that they made a mistake in calling the ancient ship the U. S. S. *Constitution*, the following letter from the Office of Naval Intelligence of the Navy Department is here reproduced.

NAVY DEPARTMENT
OFFICE OF NAVAL INTELLIGENCE
WASHINGTON

22 January 1934.

DEAR SIR:

Your letter of January 18th to the Secretary of the Navy, in which you request information as to the correct designation of the *Constitution*, has been referred to this office.

In reply, you are advised that the official designation is U. S. S. *Constitution*.

In the old days, however, she was referred to as the United States Frigate *Constitution*, and a booklet published by the Bureau of Construction and Repair of the Navy Department in 1932 is so entitled. Hence it would not be improper to use that title if you so desire.

Sincerely yours,
D. R. TALLMAN,

Dr.C. Leonard Albright,   *Lieutenant, U. S. Navy,*
University of Richmond,   *Public Relations Branch.*
Richmond, VA."

Table of Contents

Ship Cachets 1

Envelope Cachets 3

1931 (Post Office postmark) 12

1931 (*Constitution* Postal Service) 19

1932 28

1933 64

1934 140

Appendix
    Ports-Dates-Visitors 208
    Cancellation Date Checklist 212
    Harry Moore "Log" Covers 216
    "Boost Old Ironsides" Stamps 220
    Autographs 221
    USS Constitution crew list - 1931 228
    US Navy General Order No. 74 of 27 June 1908 230
        Establishing Ship Post Offices

Adm. Louis M. Nulton presiding over commissioning ceremonies
July 1, 1931

Ceremony program for commisioning of *Constitution*

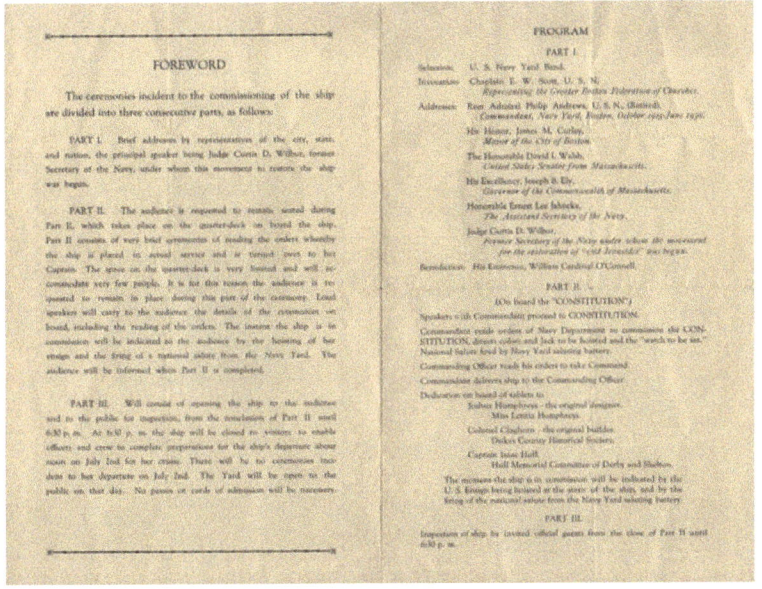

Constitution Ship Cachets

'Ship cachets' are the designs from previous Official Cachets with the dates and wording removed. These cachets were applied from time to time, by the mail clerk, on covers which did not have an official or unofficial cachet. Once made, these cachets could appear in any port and on any date and in any color. Following are the 7 available 'Ship Cachets'

Ship Cachet 1 (S1)

Modified from the Norfolk, VA cachet of October 1931
First Used at Washington, DC on April ,1932

Ship Cachet 2 (S2)

Modified from the Charleston, SC cachet of December 1931
First Used at Washington, DC on April 23, 1932

Ship Cachet 3 (S3)

Modified from the Lake Charles, LA cachet of March 1932
First Used at Washington, DC on April 23, 1932

Ship Cachet 4 (S4)

Modified from the St. Petersburg, FL cachet of April 1932
First Used at Washington, DC on July 11, 1932

Ship Cachet 5 (S5)

Modified from the Washington, DC (Navy Day) cachet of October 1932
First used at Guantanamo Bay, Cuba on December 15, 1932

Ship Cachet 6 (S6)

Modified from the San Francisco, CA cachet of September 1933
First used at San Francisco, California on September 6, 1933

Ship Cachet 7 (S7)

Modified from the San Pedro, CA cachet of February 1933
First used at San Pedro, California on October 19, 1933

Envelope Cachets

'Envelope cachets' are designs placed on the covers by individuals and organizations for use on any date at any port. These cachets are listed with the date first appearing. As these envelope cachets can be found on any date to the end of the cruise, it is therefore impossible to list every date, known or unknown, and no such attempt has been made in this book. Also, where known, the variations have also been listed and, if known, the cachet issuer will be listed. Following are the available 'Envelope Cachets'

Envelope Cachet 1 (E1)

First Used at Portsmouth, New Hampshire on July 6, 1931
Cachet issued by Everett Wallster

Envelope Cachet 2 (E2)

First Used at Yorktown, Virginia on October 19, 1931
Cachets issued by W.G Crosby

Envelope Cachet 3 (E3)

First Used at Yorktown, Virginia on October 19, 1931
Cachets issued by W.G Crosby

Envelope Cachet 4 (E4)

First Used at Yorktown, Virginia on October 19, 1931
Cachets issued by W.G Crosby

Envelope Cachet 5 (E5)

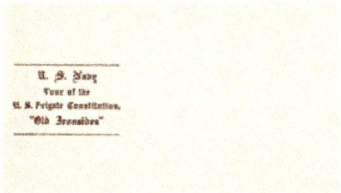

First used at Jacksonville, Florida on December 18, 1931

Envelope Cachet 6 (E6)

First used at Mobile, Alabama on January 12, 1932
Cachet was issued by A. G. Roessler

Envelope Cachet 6a (E6a)

First used at Washington, DC on April 30, 1932

Envelope Cachet 7 (E7)

First used at Washington, DC on September 17, 1932
Cachet was issued by John E. Gill

Envelope Cachet 8 (E8)

First used at Washington, DC on October 12, 1932
Cachet was issued by John E. Gill

Envelope Cachet 7a (E7a) & 8a (E8a)

Same design as 7 and 8 above except this design replaces what
is in lower right corner with **Navy Day Oct 27**
Used at Washington, DC on October 27, 1932

Envelope Cachet 8b (E8b)

Same design as 8 above except this design replaces what
is in lower right corner with **Armistice Day Nov 11**
Used at Washington, DC on November 11, 1932

Envelope Cachet 9 (E9)

First used at Guantanamo Bay, Cuba on December 15, 1932
Cachet was issued by A. C. Roessler

Envelope Cachet 10 (E10)

First used at Cristobal, Canal Zone on December 25, 1932
Cachet was issued by John e. Gill

Envelope Cachet 11 (E11)

First used at Balboa, Canal Zone on December 29, 1932
Cachet was issued by Joseph M. Hale

Envelope Cachet 10a (E10a)

First used at San Pedro, California on February 22, 1933
Cachet issued by John E. Gill

Envelope Cachet 12 (E12)

First used at San Pedro, California on February 22, 1933
Cachet issued by Argosy Stamp Club

Envelope Cachet 12a (E12a)

First used at San Pedro, California on February 22, 1933
Cachet issued by Argosy Stamp Club

Envelope Cachet 13 (E13)

First used at San Pedro, California on February 22, 1933
Cachet issued by Argosy Stamp Club

Envelope Cachet 14 (E14)

First used at San Pedro, California on February 22, 1933
Cachet issued by Argosy Stamp Club

Envelope Cachet 15 (E15)

First used at San Pedro, California on February 22, 1933
Cachet issued by Argosy Stamp Club

Envelope Cachet 16 (E16)

First used at San Pedro, California on February 22, 1933
Cachet issued by Argosy Stamp Club

Envelope Cachet 17 (E17)

First used at San Pedro, California on February 22, 1933
Cachet issued by Argosy Stamp Club

Envelope Cachet 23 (E23)

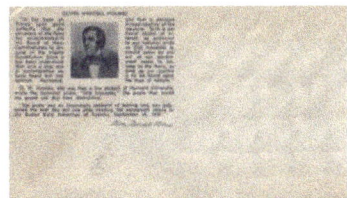

First used at San Pedro, California on February 22, 1933
Cachet issued by Argosy Stamp Club

Envelope Cachet 24 (E24)

First used at Oakland, California on April 14 22, 1933
Cachet issued by W. G. Lobdell

Envelope Cachet 25 (E25)

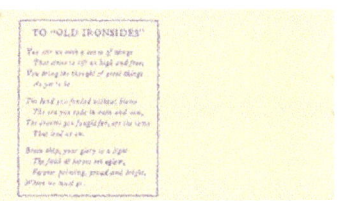

First used at Oakland, California on April 26, 1933
Cachet issued by Charles Oluf Olsen

Envelope Cachet 26 (E26)

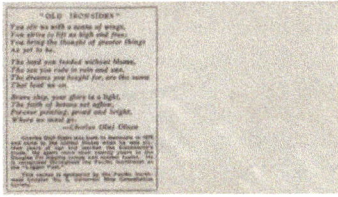

First used at Astoria, Oregon on May 13, 1933
Cachet issued by Pacific Northwest Chapter No. 2 USCS

Envelope Cachet 27 (E27)

First used at San Diego, California on February 6, 1934
Cachet issued by H. Grimeland

Envelope Cachet 18 (E18)

First used at San Pedro, California on February 22, 1933
Cachet issued by Argosy Stamp Club

Envelope Cachet 19 (E19)

First used at San Pedro, California on February 22, 1933
Cachet issued by Argosy Stamp Club

Envelope Cachet 20 (E20)

First used at San Pedro, California on February 22, 1933
Cachet issued by Argosy Stamp Club

Envelope Cachet 21 (E21)

First used at San Pedro, California on February 22, 1933
Cachet issued by Argosy Stamp Club

Envelope Cachet 22 (E22)

First used at San Pedro, California on February 22, 1933
Cachet issued by Argosy Stamp Club

Envelope Cachet 10d (E10d)

First used at San Diego, California on March 17, 1934
Cachet issued by John E. Gill

Envelope Cachet 7b (E7b)

First used at San Diego, California on March 17, 1934
Cachet issued by John E. Gill

Envelope Cachet 28 (E28)

First used at Balboa, Canal Zone on April 4, 1934
Cachet issued by Donald A. Schramm & C. Wright Richell

While this cover is not officially one of the envelope cachets, I am including it here as it is a cachet sponsored by W. G. Crosby and has shown in most all ports and with any other cachets since the *Constitution* first visited San Pedro in 1933.

Official Cachets and Private Cachets

This section will show/list "Official Cachets" and "Private Cachets"

OFFICIAL CACHETS: Those cachets sponsored free by individuals and organizations to all who sent covers. Most of the time, these cachets will only appear at a specific port, however, there may be a few exceptions.

PRIVATE CACHETS: Those cachets made up by individuals and clubs for personal use, sale, or profit. Also, those cachets for which a charge was made.

When a cachet is listed, the notation "**Official**" or "**Private**" will be noted at the beginning of each individual listing. If a specific number of envelopes with a specific cachet is known, that number will be included in the description. If the cachet sponsor, director, or designer can definitely be determined, I will list the name. Otherwise, I will designate the cachet sponsor as unknown. A list of ports visited will appear at the end of the book.

Harry Moore
Storekeeper, first class, Naval Mail Clerk on the
U.S. Frigate *Constitution*, 1931-1934

1931

BOSTON, MASSACHUSETTS: July 1, 1931 – July 2, 1931

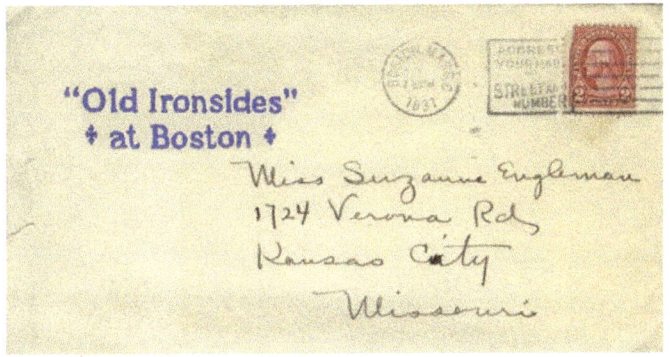

PRIVATE: Cachet sponsor Everett Wallster
First Appearance: July 1 (18 covers)

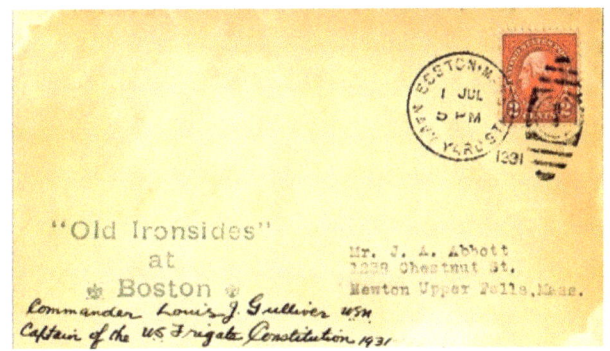

PRIVATE: Cachet sponsor Everett Wallster
First Appearance July 1 (43 covers)
NOTE: Postmark of Boston Navy Yard

GLOUCESTER, MASSACHUSETTS: July 2, 1931 – July 3, 1931

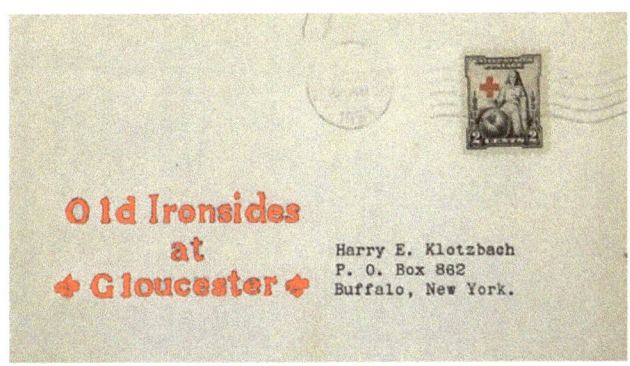

PRIVATE: Cachet sponsor Clarence Gwynne
First Appearance July 2 (2 covers)

PORTSMOUTH, NEW HAMPSHIRE: July 3, 1931 – July 12, 1931

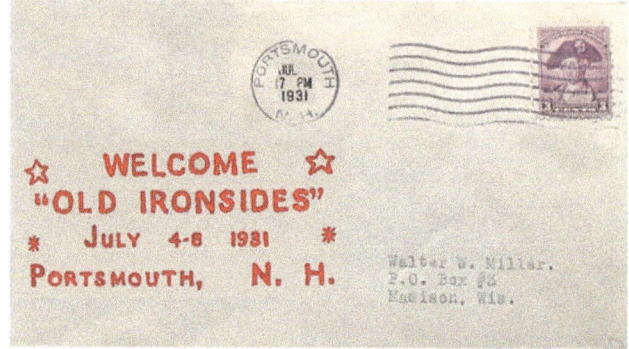

PRIVATE: Cachet sponsor Gow C. Ng

First Appearance July 4 (5 covers)

BAR HARBOR, MAINE: July 13, 1931 – July 13, 1931

PRIVATE: Cachet sponsor Everett Wallster

First Appearance July 13 (2 covers)

BATH, MAINE: July 14, 1931 – July 17, 1931

5 covers with E1 Cachet with sticker by

Bath Chamber of Commerce

PORTLAND, MAINE: July 17, 1931 – July 23, 1931

PRIVATE: Cachet sponsor Everett Wallster
First Appearance July 18 (15 covers)

GLOUCESTER, MASSACHUSETTS: July 23, 1931 – July 29, 1931

OFFICIAL: Cachet sponsor Everett Wallster
First Appearance July 29 (5 covers)

MARBLEHEAD, MASSACHUSETTS: July 29, 1931 – July 30, 1931 (No Cachet Covers)

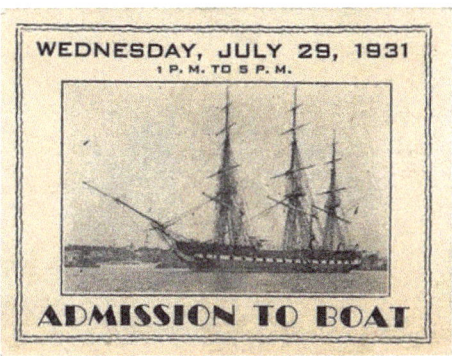

Admission ticket for access to Constitution at Marblehead, MA

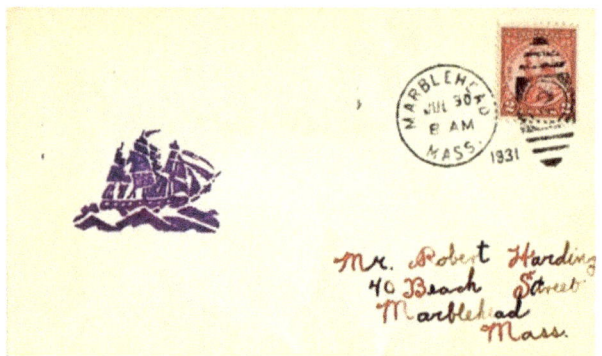

PRIVATE: Cachet sponsor unknown
First Appearance July 30 (15 covers)

NEW BEDFORD, MASSACHUSETTS: July 31, 1931 – August 6, 1931

OFFICIAL: Cachet sponsor Post 1, American Legion
First Appearance July 31 (1400 covers)

Pinback made available by Post 1, American Legion
at New Bedford, MA

16

PROVIDENCE, RHODE ISLAND: August 6, 1931 – August 10, 1931

OFFICIAL: Cachet sponsor Providence Chamber of Commerce
First Appearance August 7 (5 covers)

OFFICIAL: Cachet sponsor Providence Chamber of Commerce
First Appearance August 7 (15 covers)

OFFICIAL: Cachet sponsor Providence Chamber of Commerce
First Appearance August 10 (5 covers)

NEWPORT, RHODE ISLAND: August 10, 1931 – August 13, 1931

PRIVATE: Cachet sponsor Everett Wallster
First Appearance August 10 (12 covers)

NEW LONDON, CONNECTICUT: August 13, 1931 – August 20, 1931

OFFICIAL: Cachet sponsor Everett Wallster
First Appearance August 14 (12 covers)

MONTAUK, LONG ISLAND, NEW YORK: August 20, 1931 – August 25, 1931

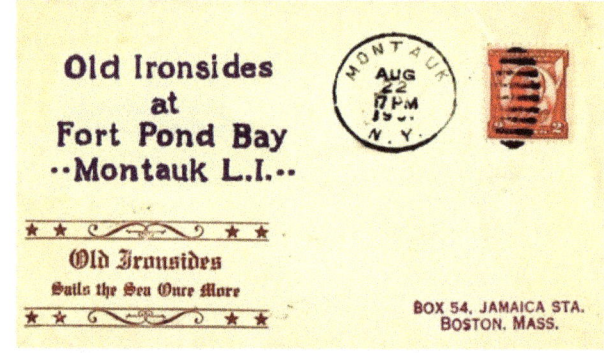

PRIVATE: Cachet sponsor Clarence Gwynne
First Appearance August 21 (4 covers)

OYSTER BAY, LONG ISLAND, NEW YORK: August 25, 1931 – August 28, 1931

OFFICIAL: Cachet sponsor Everett Wallster
First Appearance August 25 (15 covers)

NEW YORK, NEW YORK: August 29, 1931 – September 14, 1931
Also at this port: E1

PRIVATE: cachet sponsor Fordham Areo Philatelic Society
First Appearance August 29 (15 covers)

Crew USS Constitution 1932

1931
(All covers have U.S. Frigate *Constitution* Cancellations)

Starting on September 10, 1931, the U.S. Frigate *Constitution* was granted the authority to have her own Postal Service. An example of the cancellation is below. The name "U.S. Frigate *Constitution*" with the date and time will be in the cancellation circle. The name of the port (or location) will be in the "killer bars." Also, since the U.S. Frigate *Constitution* Postal Service was instituted, many of the covers from various ports will only bear the cancellation with no cachet.

NEW YORK, NEW YORK: August 29, 1931 – September 14, 1931
Also at this port: E1
KILLER BARS: New York
              NY

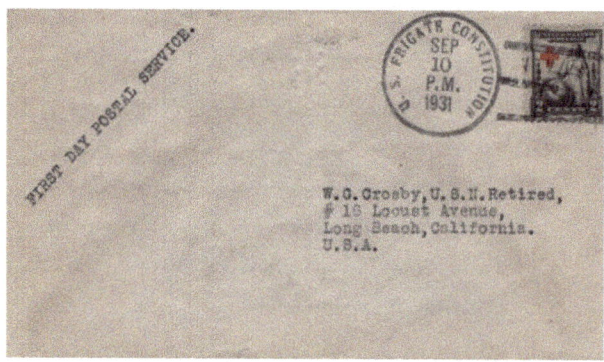

OFFICIAL: First Day Postal Service
First Appearance September 10

NOTE: Harry Moore had been appointed as Mail Clerk on the *Constitution*, however, because of his absence from the ship, the cancellations applied on Sept. 10, were applied by another individual. It may be assumed that F. A. Majerowski performed these duties as he filled in for Moore when he was later unavailable. The next date canceled on the *Constitution* was Sept. 14 which are attributed to Moore.

NEWPORT NEWS, VIRGINIA: October 2, 1931 – October 9, 1931
Also at this port: E1
KILLER BARS: NEWPORT
　　　　　　　　NEWS, VA.

First Appearance October 2

NORFORK, VIRGINIA: October 9, 1931 – October 16, 1931
Also at this port: E1
KILLER BARS: NORFOLK
　　　　　　　　VA.

OFFICIAL: Cachet sponsor Norfolk-Portsmouth Chamber Commerce
First Appearance October 9

OFFICIAL: Cachet sponsor Norfolk Rotary Club
First Appearance October 9

WILMINGTON, DELAWARE: September 16, 1931 – September 18, 1931
Also at this port: E1
KILLER BARS: WILMINGTON
                         DEL.

First Appearance September 16

PHILADELPHIA, PENNSYLVANIA: September 18, 1931 – October 1, 1931
Also at this port: E1
KILLER BARS: PHILA.
                         PA

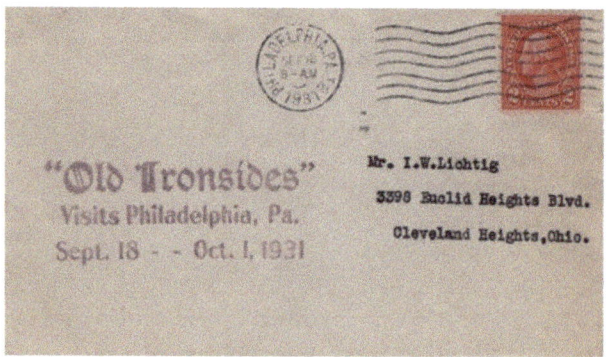

OFFICIAL: Cachet sponsor David E. Cook
All covers with this cachet were postmarked in the
Philadelphia Post Office
First Appearance September 18

WARNING: Charles Albright issued the following: "The collector of Old Ironsides covers is warned to be on the lookout for covers canceled at Norfolk in November, 1931. These spurious covers have "Norfolk Nav. Base" in the killer bars. The ship was not at this place and the covers are therefore deemed fraudulent."

YORKTOWN, VIGINIA: October 16, 1931 – October 23, 1931
Also at this port: E1, E2, E3, E4
KILLER BARS: YORKTOWN,
                          VA

The above print of President Hoover appears on many covers of October 19, 1931 (May also be different type styles)

BALTIMORE, MARYLAND: October 24, 1931 – November 2, 1931
Also at this port: E1, E2
KILLER BARS: BALTIMORE
                          MD.

First Appearance October 24

KILLER BARS: BALTIMORE
                          NAVY DAY

First Appearance October 27

ANNAPOLIS, MARYLAND: November 2, 1931 – November 5, 1931
Also at this port: E1, E3
KILLER BARS: ANNAPOLIS
                          MD.

First Appearance November 2

QUANTICO, VIRGINIA: November 6, 1931 – November 7, 1931
KILLER BARS: QUANTICO
                          VA.

First Appearance November 7

WASHINGTON, DC: November 7 1931 – November 18, 1931
Also at this port: E1, E3, E4
KILLER BARS: WASHINGTON
                          DC.

First Appearance November 7

PRIVATE: Cachet sponsor W. G. Crosby
First Appearance November 11

WILMINGTON, NORTH CAROLINA: Nov 21, 1931 – Nov 30, 1931
Also at this port: E1
KILLER BARS: WILMINGTON
NC

OFFICIAL: Cachet sponsor Chamber of Commerce
First Appearance November 21

KILLER BARS: THANKSGIVING
DAY.

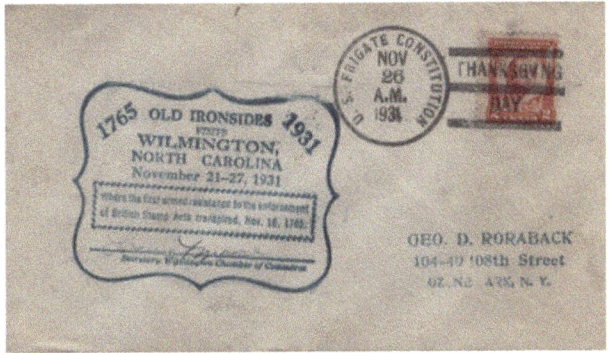

OFFICIAL: Cachet sponsor Chamber of Commerce
First Appearance November 26

CHARLESTON, SOUTH CAROLINA: December 1, 1931 – December 6, 1931
KILLER BARS: CHARLESTON
                SC

First Appearance December 1

SAVANNAH, GEORGIA: December 7, 1931 – December 11, 1931
KILLER BARS: SAVANNAH
                GA.

PRIVATE: Cachet sponsor Chamber of Commerce
First Appearance December 7

BRUNSWICK, GEORGIA: Dec. 12, 1931 – Dec. 15, 1931
KILLER BARS: BRUNSWICK
                GA.

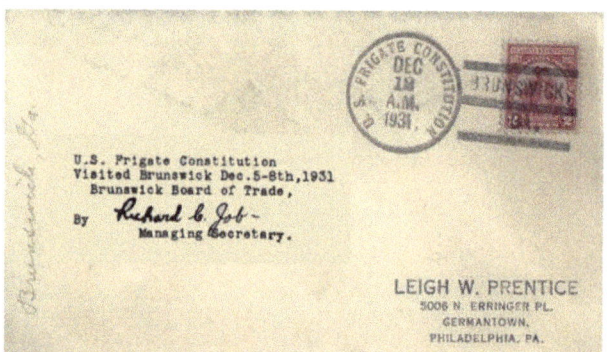

OFFICIAL: Cachet sponsor Brunswick Board of Trade
First Appearance December 12

JACKSONVILLE, FLORIDA: Dec. 16, 1931 – Dec. 21, 1931
Also at this port: E5
KILLER BARS: JACKSONVILLE
                FLA.

First Appearance December 16

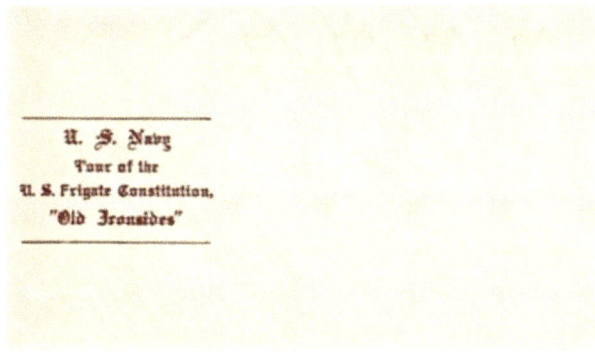

First Appearance Envelope Cachet E5 December 18

MIAMI, FLORIDA: December 23, 1931 – December 30, 1931
KILLER BARS: MIAMI
                FLA

OFFICIAL: Cachet sponsor Chamber of Commerce
First Appearance December 23

KILLER BARS: MIAMI, FLA
MERRY XMAS

First Appearance December 25

KEY WEST, FLORIDA: December 31, 1931 – January 4, 1932
Also at this port: S1
KILLER BARS: KEY WEST,
FLA.

First Appearance December 31

KILLER BARS: KEY WEST
FLA. H.N.Y.

Note: The January 1st covers with H.N.Y. in the bars means Happy New Year

1932

PENSACOLA, FLORIDA: January 6, 1932 – January 11, 1932
KILLER BARS: PENSACOLA
         FLA

OFFICIAL: Cachet sponsor Chamber of Commerce
First Appearance January 7

MOBILE, ALABAMA: January 11, 1932 – January 18, 1932
Also at this port: E5, E6
KILLER BARS: MOBILE
         ALA.

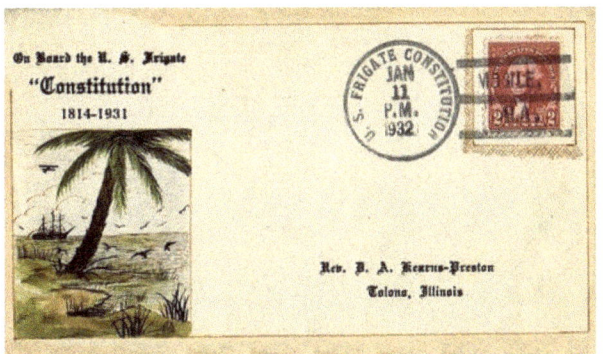

PRIVATE: Cachet sponsor unknown
First Appearance January 11

OFFICIAL: Cachet sponsor unknown
First Appearance January 11

OFFICIAL: Cachet sponsor Chamber of Commerce
First Appearance January 12

First Appearance Envelope cachet E6 January 12

OFFICIAL: Cachet sponsor Chamber of Commerce
First Appearance January 15

BATON ROUGE, LOUISIANA: Jan 20, 1932 – Jan 27, 1932
Also at this port: S1
KILLER BARS: BATON ROUGE, LA.

First Appearance January 20

NEW ORLEANS: January 27, 1932 – February 12, 1932
Also at this port: S1, E1, E6
KILLER BARS: NEW ORLEANS, LA.

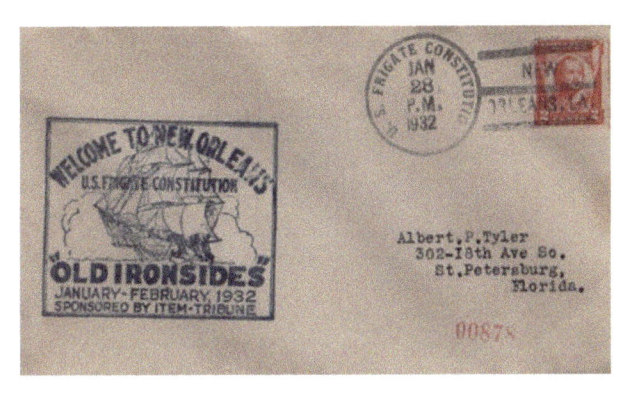

OFFICIAL: Cachet sponsor The New Orleans Item-Tribune
First Appearance January 27

OFFICIAL: Cachet sponsor Crescent City Post No. 125, American Legion
First Appearance January 28

KILLER BARS: New ORL'NS
　　　　　　　　MARDI GRAS

OFFICIAL: Cachet sponsor Aereo Philatelic Club
First Appearance February 9 (833 Covers)

KILLER BARS: NEW ORL'NS
　　　　　　　　LA.

First Appearance February 9

OFFICIAL: Cachet sponsor Chamber of Commerce
First Appearance 17

NOTE: The date "16th" removed from the cachet and that cachet used on all dates at this port. Many covers have the current date applied to the cachet with the cancel date.

PRIVATE: Cachet sponsor Chamber of Commerce
First Appearance February 22

Constitution approaching the bascule bridge Corpus Christi, TX

ENROUTE TO CORPUS CRISTI, TEXAS
KILLER BARS: LINCOLN'S
BIRTHDAY

First Appearance February 12

NOTE: Most of the covers are back-stamped Corpus Christi, February 14th and have New Orleans cachets.

CORPUS CHRISTI, TEXAS: Feb 14, 1932 – Feb 23, 1932
Also at this port: S1, E1
KILLER BARS: CORPUS
CHRISTI, TEX

OFFICIAL: Cachet sponsor Chamber of Commerce
First Appearance February 16

GALVESTON, TEXAS
KILLER BARS: GALVESTON
                      TEXAS

First Appearance February 24

NOTE: The *Constitution* on the way to Houston, Texas, made this unscheduled stop in Galveston, and departed early the next day. There was some doubt about the Frigate's towering masts clearing the wires that crossed over the Houston Ship Channel. The uncertainty of docking the ship late at night at Houston caused this stop over. The Chairman of the Galveston Committee came aboard. Later, the Reception Committee from Galveston and Houston came aboard. No other visitors while at this port. There were only a very small number of envelopes canceled with the February 24 date to commemorate this stop. All covers have the Houston cancel date of February 25 on the opposite side.

HOUSTON, TEXAS: February 25, 1932 – March 1, 1932
Also at this port: E1
KILLER BARS: HOUSTON
                      TEXAS.

OFFICIAL: Cachet sponsor Chamber of Commerce
First Appearance February 26 (1000 covers)

GALVESTON, TEXAS: March 1, 1932 – March 7, 1932
Also at this port: E1
KILLER BARS: GALVESTON
TEXAS

OFFICIAL: Cachet sponsor Chamber of Commerce
First Appearance March 1

BEAUMONT, TEXAS: March 8, 1932 – March 12, 1932
KILLER BARS: BEAUMONT
TEXAS

OFFICIAL: Cachet sponsor Chamber of Commerce
First Appearance March 8

PORT ARTHUR: March 12, 1932 – March 17, 1932
KILLER BARS: PORT ARTHUR
                          TEXAS

First Appearance March 12

ORANGE, TEXAS: March 17, 1932 – March 19, 1932
KILLER BARS: ORANGE
                          TEXAS

First Appearance March 17

LAKE CHARLES: March 19, 1932 – March 22, 1932
KILLER BARS: LAKE
                          CHAS., LA.

OFFICIAL: Cachet sponsor The Lake Charles Association of Commerce - First Appearance March 19

GULFPORT, MISSISSIPPI: March 25, 1932 - March 29, 1932
Also at this port: S1, E1, E6
KILLER BARS: GULFPORT
                MISS

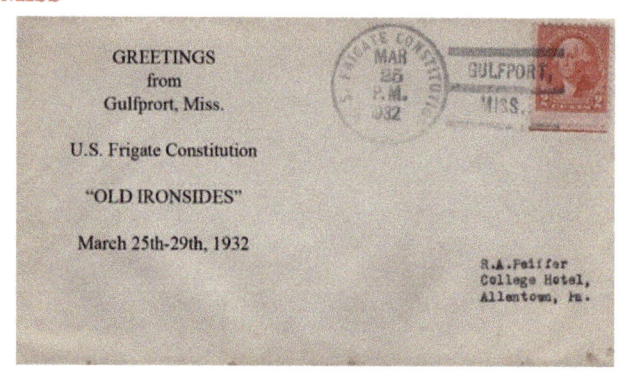

OFFICIAL: Cachet sponsor Forty-and-Eight
First Appearance March 25

OFFICIAL: Cachet sponsor unknown
First Appearance March 25

WARNING: There has been found that there were fraudulent covers mailed from Gulfport. These date from January 15th to January 31st inclusive.

PORT SAINT JOE, FLORIDA: March 30, 1932 – April 1, 1932
Also at this port: S1
KILLER BARS: PORT ST. JOE
                     FLA

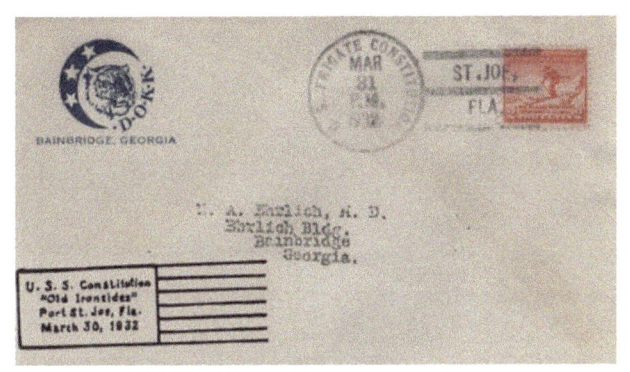

OFFICIAL: Cachet sponsor unknown
First Appearance March 30

TAMPA, FLORIDA: April 3, 1932 – April 7, 1932
KILLER BARS: TAMPA
                     FLA.

OFFICIAL: Cachet sponsor Chamber of Commerce
First Appearance April 3

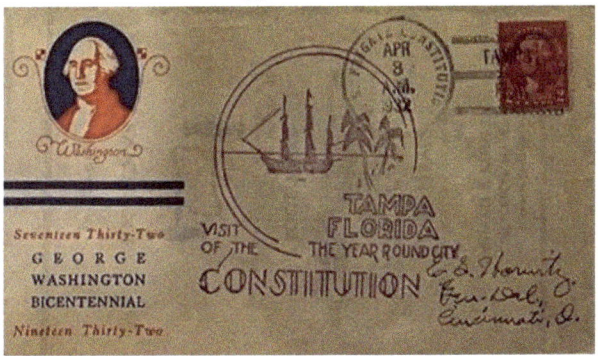

OFFICIAL: Cachet sponsor unknown
First Appearance April 3

ST. PETERSBURG, FLORIDA: April 7, 1932 – April 9, 1932
Also at this port: E2, E4
KILLER BARS: ST. PETERS-
   BURG, FLA.

OFFICIAL: Cachet sponsor Chamber of Commerce
First Appearance April 7

WASHINGTON, DC: April 16, 1932 – May 11, 1932
Also at this port: E6, E6a
KILLER BARS: WASHINGTON
   DC

First Appearance April 16

First Appearance Ship Cachet S1 - April 23

First Appearance Ship Cachet S2 - April 23

First Appearance Ship Cachet S3 - April 23

PRIVATE: Cachet sponsor unknown
First Appearance April 30

President Hoover tours the *Constitution* - 1931

ALEXANDRIA, VIRGINIA: May 11, 1932 – May 12, 1932
Also at this port: S1, S3
KILLER BARS: ALEXANDRIA
                        VA.

First Appearance May 12

PRIVATE: Cachet sponsor John Dunlop
(An envelope with this cache is unavailable)
First Appearance May 12

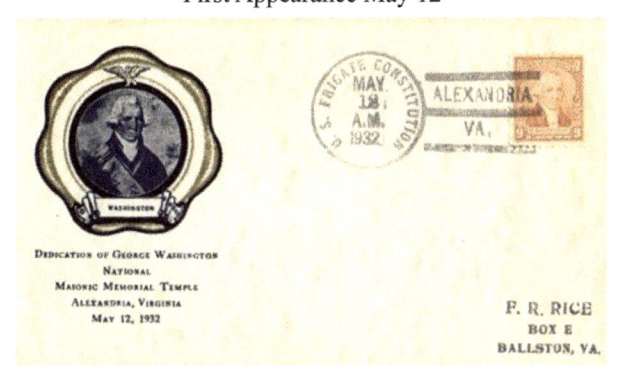

PRIVATE: Cachet sponsor unknown
First Appearance June 24

WASHINGTON, DC: May 12, 1932 – December 8, 1932
Also at this port: S1, S2, S3, E6
KILLER BARS: WASHINGTON
DC

PRIVATE: Cachet sponsor unknown
First Appearance June 16

PRIVATE: Cachet sponsor unknown
First Appearance June 24

PRIVATE: Cachet sponsor unknown
First Appearance June 24

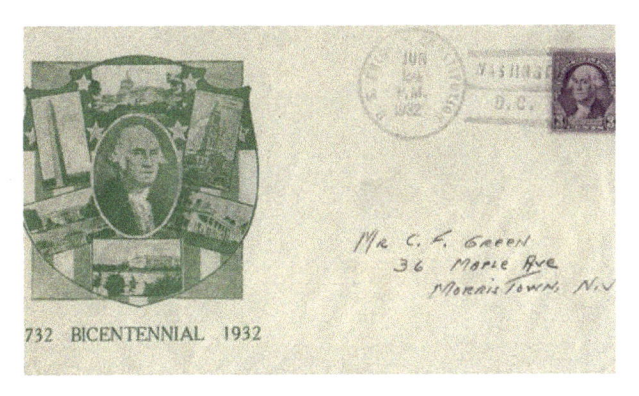

PRIVATE: Cachet sponsor unknown
First Appearance June 24

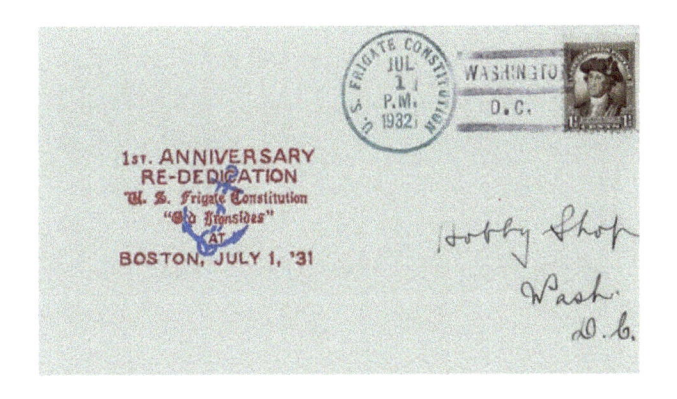

PRIVATE: Cachet sponsor John E. Gill
First Appearance July 1

PRIVATE: Cachet sponsor Joseph M. Hale & Everett Wallster
First Appearance July 1

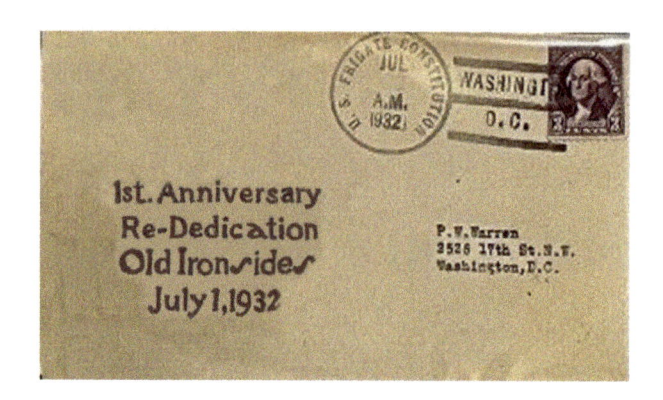

PRIVATE: Cachet sponsor The Fairway Cover Service
First Appearance July 1

PRIVATE: Cachet sponsor Unknown
First Appearance July 4

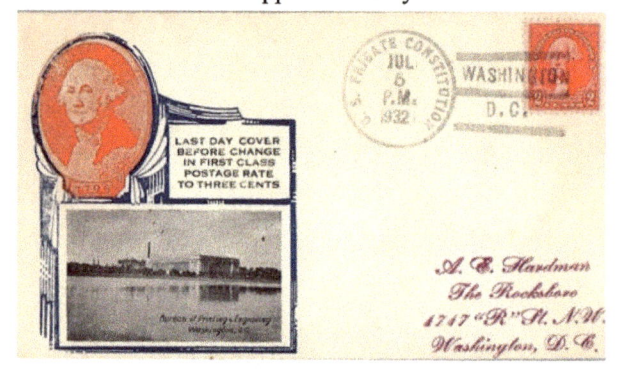

PRIVATE: Cachet sponsor Unknown
First Appearance July 5

PRIVATE: Cachet sponsor Unknown
First Appearance July 25

PRIVATE: Cachet sponsor Unknown
First Appearance July 25

First Appearance 'Ship Cachet' S4 July 26

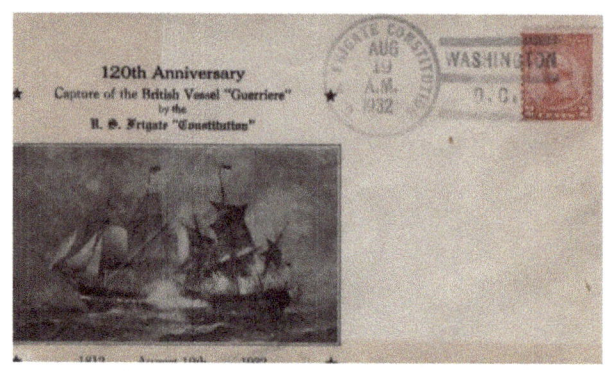

PRIVATE: Cachet sponsor Everett Wallster & Joseph M. Hale
First Appearance August 19

PRIVATE: Cachet sponsor John E. Gill
First Appearance August 19

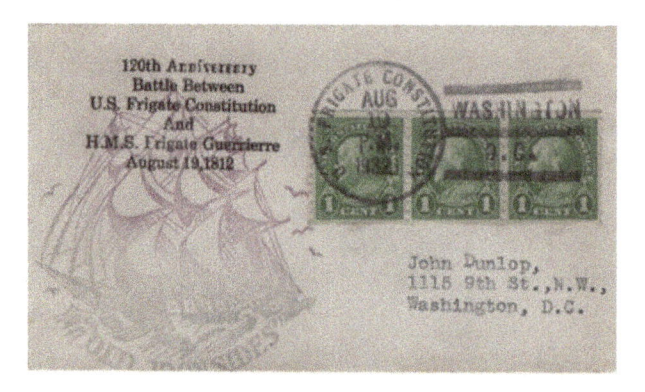

PRIVATE: Cachet sponsor Elmer Nelson
First Appearance August 19

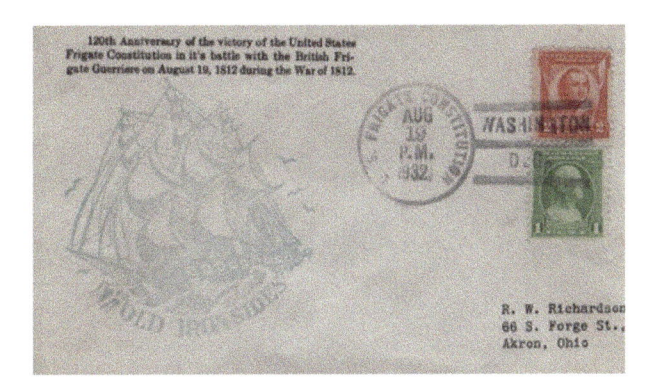

PRIVATE: Cachet sponsor R.W. Richardson
First Appearance August 19

PRIVATE: Cachet sponsor unknown
First Appearance August 19

PRIVATE: Cachet sponsor Everett Wallster & J. M. Hale
First Appearance September 17

OFFICIAL: Cachet sponsor John Gill
First Appearance Envelope Cachet E7 September 17

OFFICIAL: Cachet sponsor John Gill
First Appearance Envelope Cachet E8 October 12

PRIVATE: Cachet sponsor unknown
First Appearance October 12

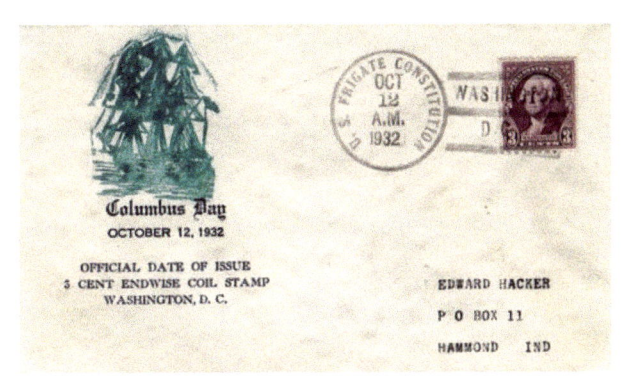

PRIVATE: Cachet sponsor unknown
First Appearance October 12

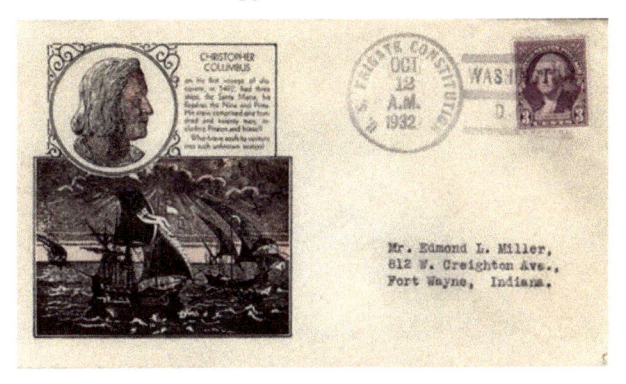

PRIVATE: Cachet sponsor unknown
First Appearance October 12

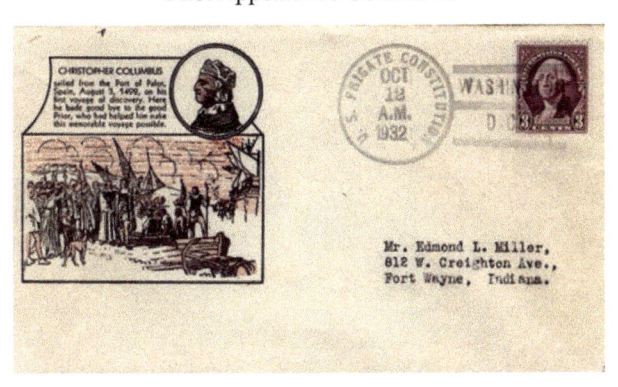

PRIVATE: Cachet sponsor unknown
First Appearance October 12

PRIVATE: Cachet sponsor Everett Wallster & Joseph M. Hale
First Appearance October 19

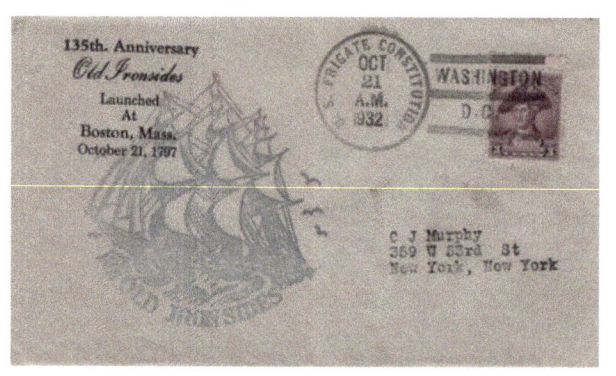

PRIVATE: Cachet sponsor W. N. Marshall
First Appearance October 21

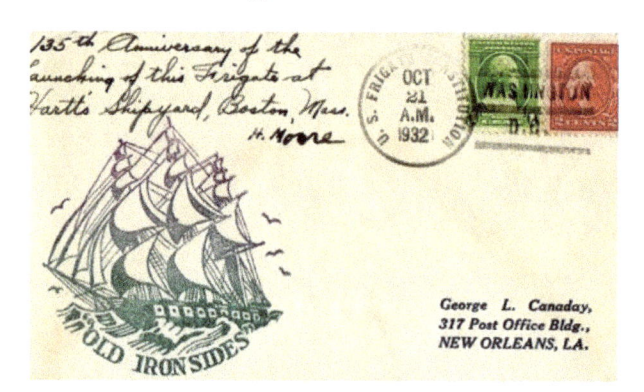

PRIVATE: Cachet sponsor Harry Moore
First Appearance October 21

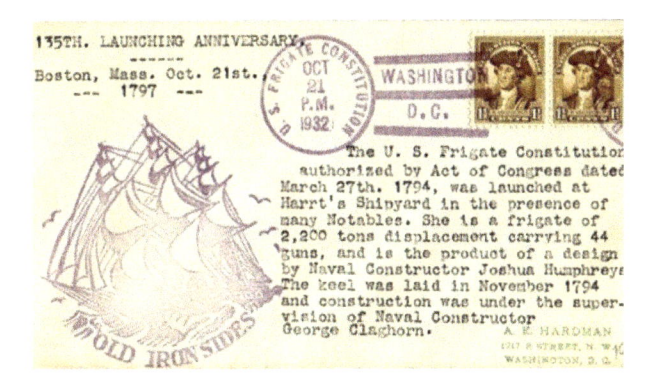

PRIVATE: Cachet sponsor A. E. Hardman
First Appearance October 21

PRIVATE: Cachet sponsor unknown
First Appearance October 24

PRIVATE: Cachet sponsor unknown
First Appearance October 25

PRIVATE: Cachet sponsor unknown
First Appearance October 25

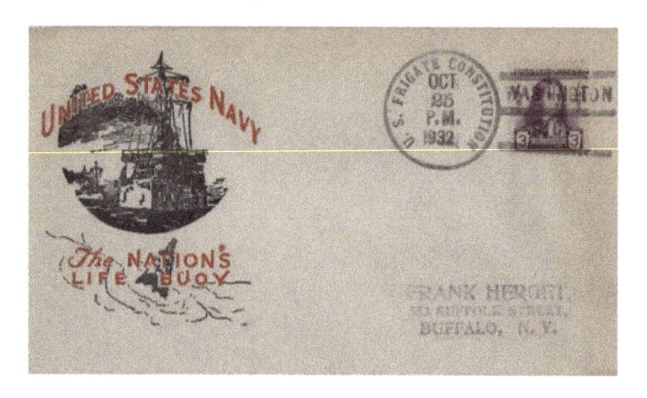

PRIVATE: Cachet sponsor unknown
First Appearance October 25

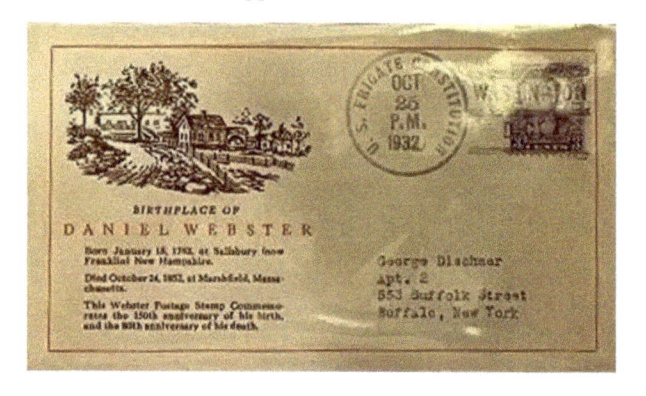

PRIVATE: Cachet sponsor unknown
First Appearance October 25

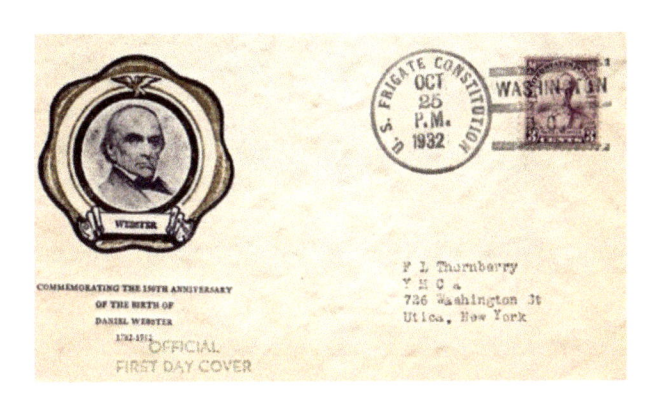

PRIVATE: Cachet sponsor unknown
First Appearance October 25

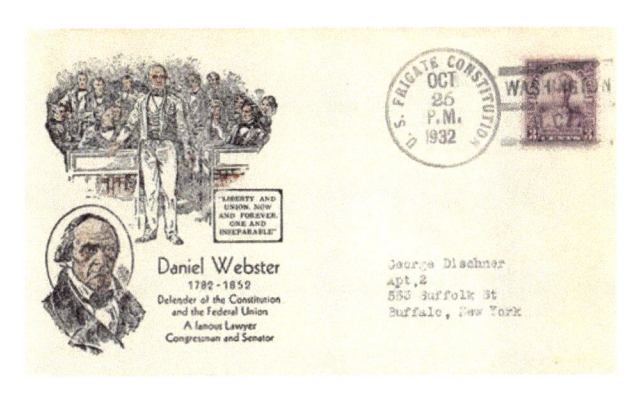

PRIVATE: Cachet sponsor unknown
First Appearance October 25

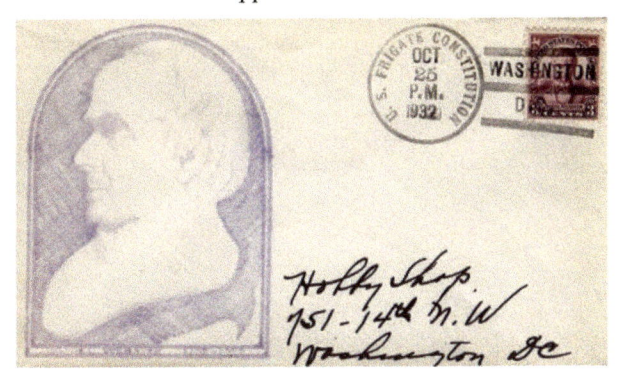

PRIVATE: Cachet sponsor unknown
First Appearance October 25

PRIVATE: Cachet sponsor John E. Gill
First Appearance October 25

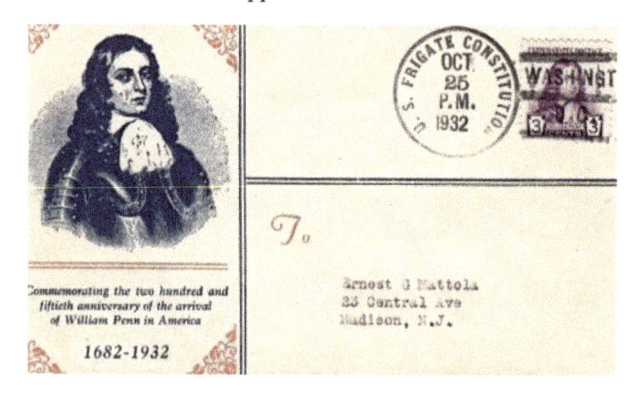

PRIVATE: Cachet sponsor unknown
First Appearance October 25

OFFICIAL: Cachet sponsor George Washington
Bicentennial Committee
First Appearance October 27

KILLER BARS: WASHINGTON DC
                  NAVY DAY

OFFICIAL: Cachet sponsor George Washington Bicentennial Committee
First Appearance October 27

KILLER BARS: WASHINGTON
                  DC

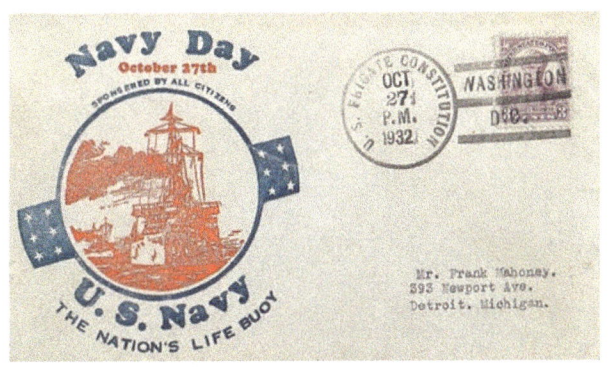

PRIVATE: Cachet sponsor unknown
First Appearance October 27

OFFICIAL: Cachet sponsor John Gill
First Appearance Envelope Cachet E7a & E8a October 27
(Same as E7 & E8 but with **NAVY DAY OCT 27** in lower right corner)

56

OFFICIAL: Cachet sponsor John Gill
First Appearance Envelope Cachet E8b November 11

PRIVATE: Cachet sponsor unknown
First Appearance November 11

PRIVATE: Cachet sponsor unknown
First Appearance November 11

PRIVATE: Cachet sponsor unknown
First Appearance November 11

PRIVATE: Cachet sponsor unknown
First Appearance November 24

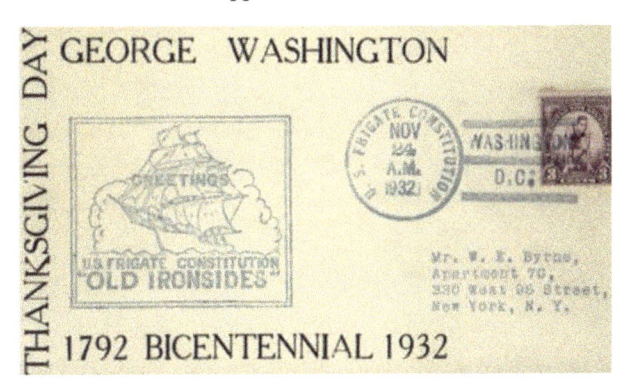

PRIVATE: Cachet sponsor unknown
First Appearance November 24

PRIVATE: Cachet sponsor unknown
First Appearance November 24

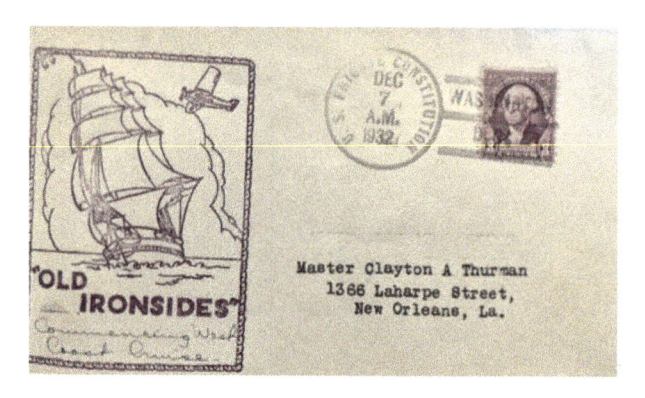

OFFICIAL: Cachet sponsor unknown
First Appearance December 7 (400 covers)

Note: Written at the bottom of the cachet "Commencing West Coast Cruise, H.M." December 7th was to have been the last day at Washington, but because of unfavorable weather conditions off Cape Hatteras, it was decided to postpone the departure until the next morning, December 8th.

GUANTANAMO BAY, CUBA: Dec 14, 1932 – Dec 19, 1932
Also know at this port: S1, S2, S3, S4, E7, E8
KILLER BARS: GUANTANAMO
                 CUBA

NOTE: There are covers with possible Cuban town cancellations.

First appearance of the 'Ship Cachets' (S5) December 15

OFFICIAL: Cachet sponsor A. C. Roessler
First appearance of the Envelope Cachet E9 December 15

CRISTOBAL, CANAL ZONE: Dec 22, 1932 – Dec 27, 1932
Also Known at this port: E7, E8, S2, S4, S5
KILLER BARS: CRISTOBAL
                      CANAL ZONE

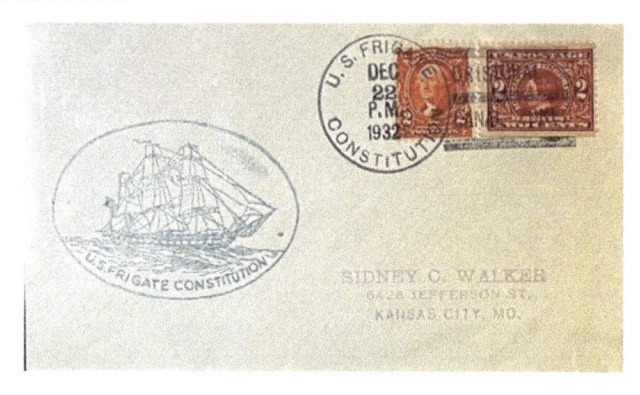

First Appearance December 22

PRIVATE: Cachet sponsor unknown
First appearance December 25

First appearance of the Envelope Cachet E10 December 25

NOTE: Cachet E10 is used with various borders in Red, Green and Gold, also E10 cachet words used with cuts of Santa and other centers.

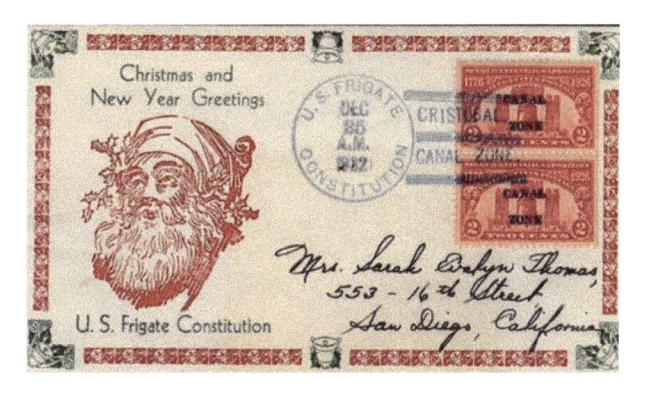

PRIVATE: Cachet sponsor unknown
First appearance December 25

PRIVATE: Cachet sponsor unknown
First appearance December 25

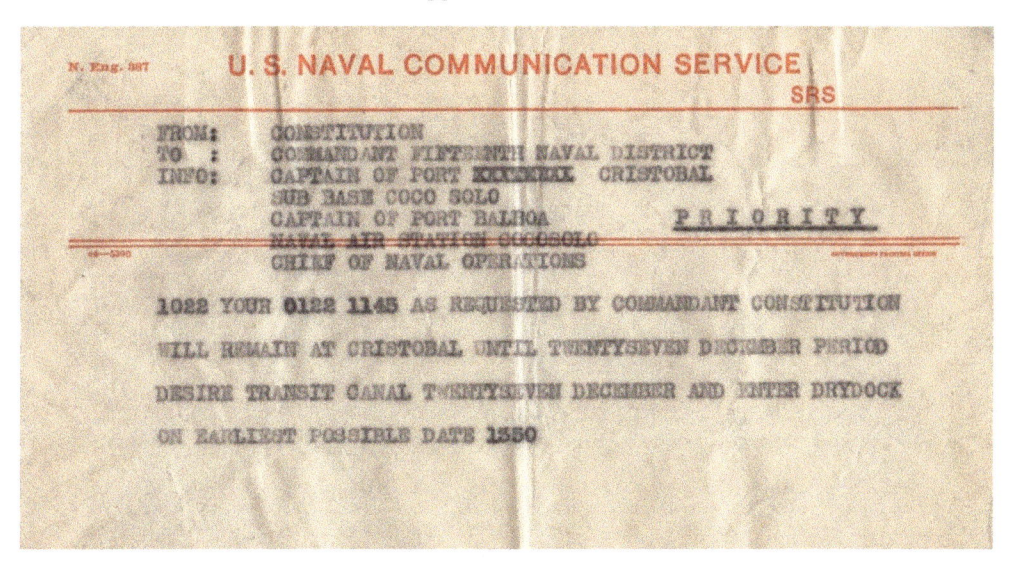

Communication with Constitution to remain in Cristobal,
then transit Canal and enter dry dock

BALBOA, CANAL ZONE: Dec 27, 1932 – Jan 7, 1933
Also know are S1, S2, S3, S4, S5, E7, E8, E10
KILLER BARS: BALBOA
             CANAL ZONE

First appearance of the Envelope Cachet E11   December 29

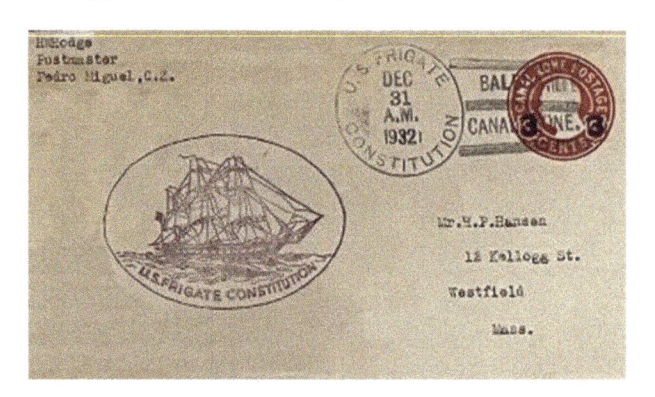

First Appearance Dcember 22

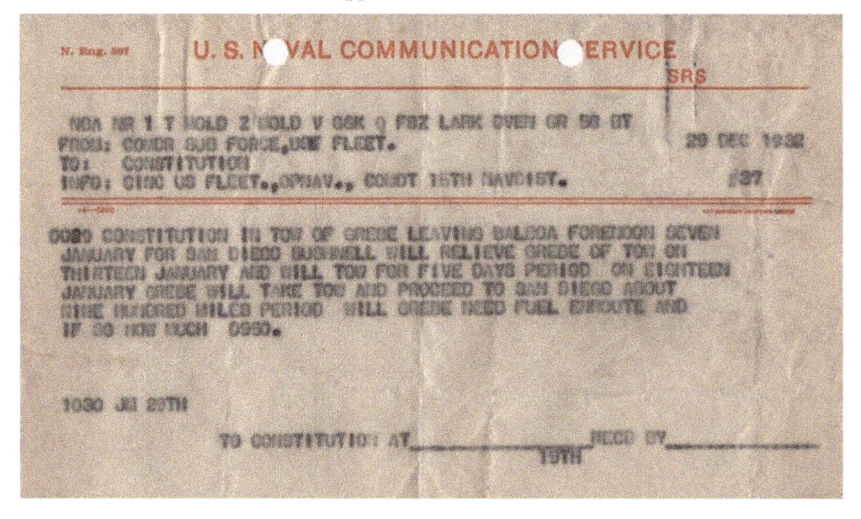

Communication to Constitution at Balboa, Canal Zone

1933

ENROUTE TO SAN DIEGO, CALIFORNIA:
KILLER BARS: LAT. 10-48 N
LONG. 87-18 W

S4 with date January 10

KILLER BARS: LAT. 14-49 N
LONG. 92-53 W

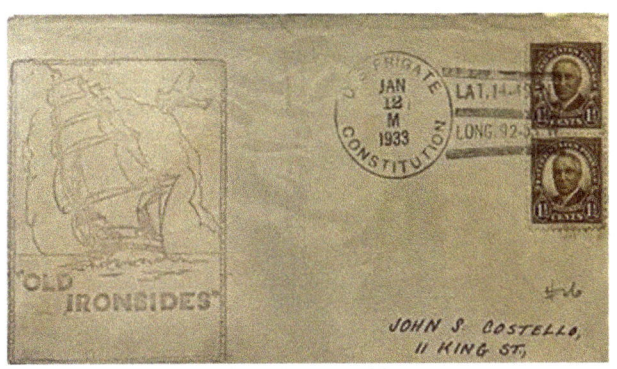

Date January 12

KILLER BARS: LAT. 15-19 N
LONG. 96-12 W

S5 with Date January 13

64

KILLER BARS: **LAT. 16-22 N**
LONG. 99-24 W

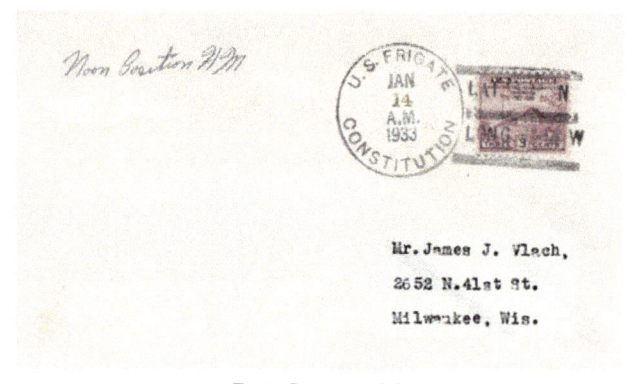

Date January 14

KILLER BARS: **LAT. 18-03 N**
LONG. 103-10 W

Date January 15

KILLER BARS: **LAT. 25-05 N**
LONG. 113-09

S3 with date January 18

SAN DIEGO, CALIFORNIA: Jan 21, 1933 – February 16, 1933
Also at this port: S1, S2, S3, S4, E7
KILLER BARS: SAN DIEGO
                CALIFORNIA

OFFICIAL: Cachet sponsor H. M. Brehm
First Appearance January 21

OFFICIAL: Cachet sponsor H. M. Brehm
First Appearance January 21

OFFICIAL: Cachet sponsor H. M. Breh
First Appearance January 25

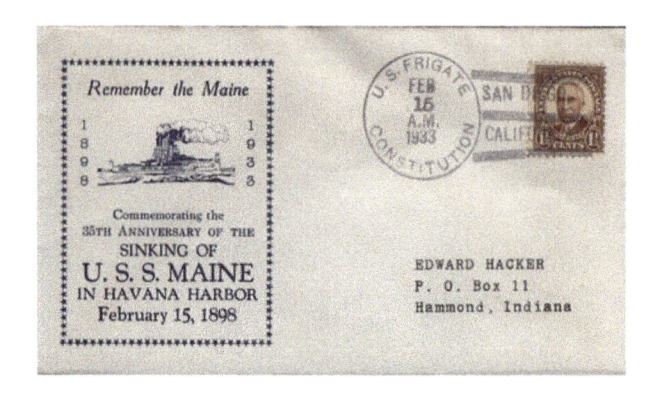

67

PRIVATE: Cachet Sponsor unknown
First Appearance February 17

Handout given to visitors at San Pedro

SAN PEDRO, CALIFORNIA: Feb 17, 1933 – March 10, 1933
Also at this port: S1, S2, S3, S4, S5, E7, E8
KILLER BARS: SAN PEDRO
                 CALIFORNIA

OFFICIAL: Cachet sponsor San Pedro Chamber of Commerce
First Appearance February 17
NOTE: same cover as above was also canceled on March 2, but with the Lion's Club print in brown

PRIVATE: Cachet sponsor unknown
First Appearance February 17

OFFICIAL: Cachet sponsor San Pedro Chamber of Commerce
First Appearance February 22

68

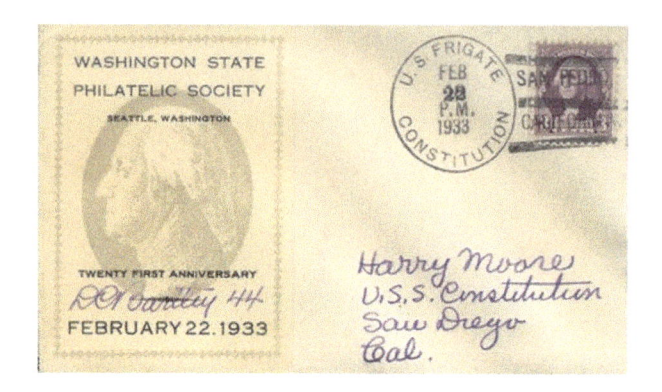

PRIVATE: Cachet sponsor Washington State Philatelic Society
First Appearance February 22

First Appearance E10a February 22

OFFICIAL: Cachet sponsor San Pedro Chamber of Commerce
First Appearance March 4

OFFICIAL: Cachet sponsor San Pedro Chamber of Commerce
First Appearance March 4

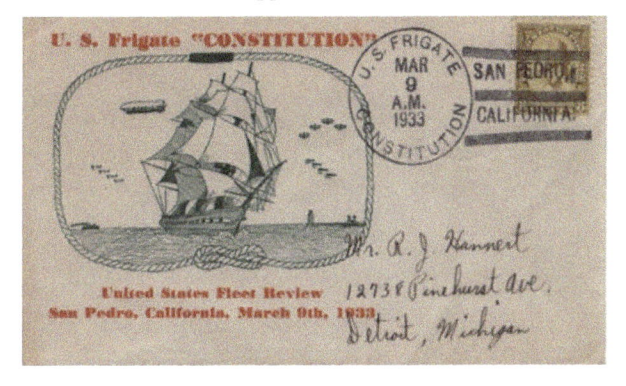

OFFICIAL: Cachet sponsor San Pedro Chamber of Commerce
First Appearance March 9

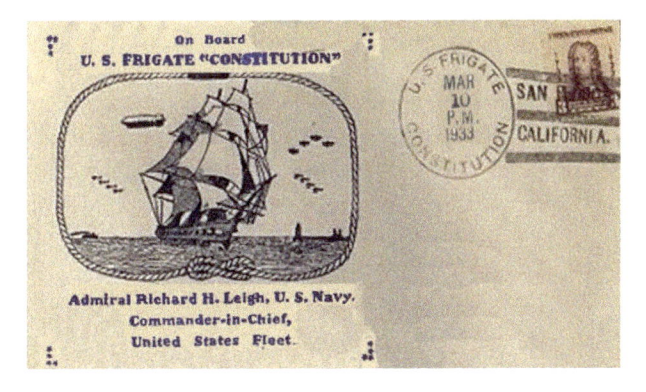

OFFICIAL: Cachet sponsor San Pedro Chamber of Commerce
First Appearance March 10

NOTE: There are two covers of this design on this date. The difference between them is the size of the type.

NOTE: A special cachet envelope was issued by the Argosy Stamp Club of the Cathederal High School, Los Angeles. It showed a reproduction of the *Constitution* from the book "The Frigate *Constitution*" by Ira N. Hollis.

Later a set of twelve special printed envelopes (printed in blue) were issued. The E12 cachet was used with a smaller type for the wording, together with other photographs and paintings, reproduced through permission of the Navy Department and other copyright owners including some from the book of Ira N. Hollis.

Mr. Gweald M. Breen was President of the Argosy Stamp Club and Brother Claudius Anthony was Director and Faculty Advisor.

To save space in this book, the Envelope cachets E12 - E23 will not be reproduced here but can be found at the beginning of this book and were fist introduced on February 22.

Envelope cachet 12

Envelope cachet 12a

LONG BEACH, CALIFORNIA; March 10, 1933 – March 19, 1933
Also at this port: S1, S2, S3, S4, S5, E10a, E12
KILLER BARS: LONG BEACH
                   CALIFORNIA

OFFICIAL: Cachet sponsor Chamber of Commerce
First Appearance March 10

OFFICIAL: Cachet sponsor Byrd L. Powell
First Appearance March 10

OFFICIAL: Cachet sponsor Byrd L. Powell
First Appearance March 10

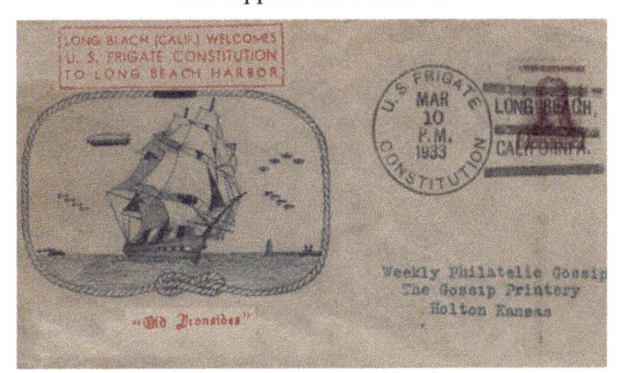

First Appearance E10b March 17

PRIVATE: Cachet sponsor unknown
First Appearance March 17

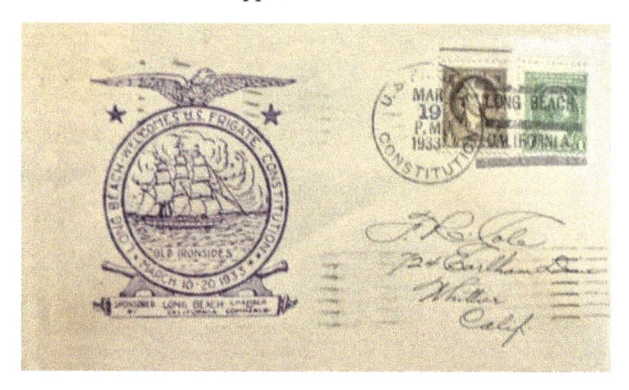

OFFICIAL: Cachet sponsor Chamber of Commerce
First Appearance March 19

NOTE: This cachet has same design as previous, except a bit smaller in size. Also, there will be three of these cachets on a single envelope in the following combinations.
Red, Green, Blue - Purple, Green, Red - Purple, Green, Blue - Purple, Red, Blue

HISTORICAL NOTE: On March 10th, an earthquake occurred at Long Beach. Harry Moore, Mail Clerk, took the 2,500 covers to the Post Office where these covers were backstamped and mailed at 4:00 P.M. At 5:54 P.M., The quake occurred and the two postal clerks who had helped backstamp the covers a short time before were both killed when the Long Beach Post Office was damaged.

Long Beach Post Office after earthquake

SANTA BARBARA, CALIFORNIA:
NOTE: Scheduled to stop at this port on March 20, 1933, but due to rough seas, no stop was made. However, Old Ironsides lay for about two hours off this port, no mail being canceled on ship or sent ashore. To fulfill the requested cachets, those covers were canceled at the next stop. Thus the Santa Barbara, March 20 cachet and San Francisco in the Killer Bars.

KILLER BARS: SAN FRANCIS-
                     CO, CALIF.

OFFICIAL: Cachet sponsor Chamber of Commerce

SAN FRANCISCO, CALIFORNIA: March 24, 1933 – April 12, 1933
Also at this port: S1, S3, S5, E7, E9, E10a, E12
KILLER BARS: SAN FRANCIS-
                     CO., CALIF.

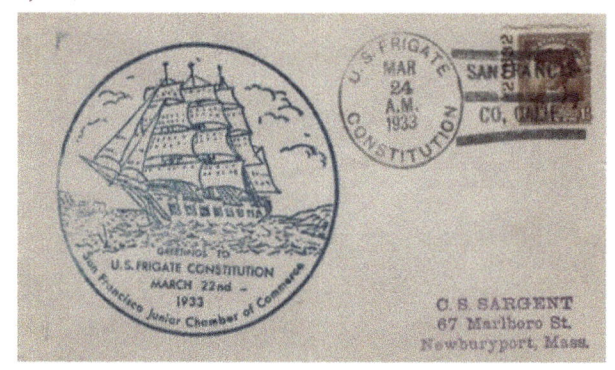

OFFICIAL: Cachet sponsor Junior Chamber of Commerce
First Appearance March 24 (9,310 covers)

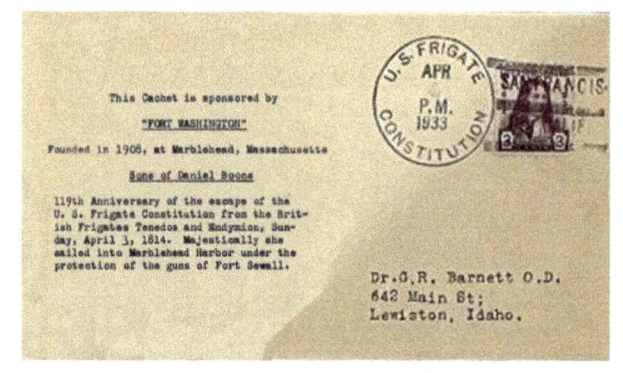

PRIVATE: Cachet sponsor Frank I. Morse
First Appearance April 3

PRIVATE: Cachet sponsor unknown
First Appearance April 10

OAKLAND, CALIFORNIA: April 12, 1933 – April 26, 1933
Also at this port: **S1, S2, S3, S5, E9, E10a, E11, E12**
KILLER BARS: OAKLAND
 CALIFORNIA

OFFICIAL: Cachet sponsor Chamber of Commerce
First Appearance April 12 (1,500 covers)

First Appearance E24 April 14

76

PRIVATE: Cachet sponsor unknown
First Appearance April 19

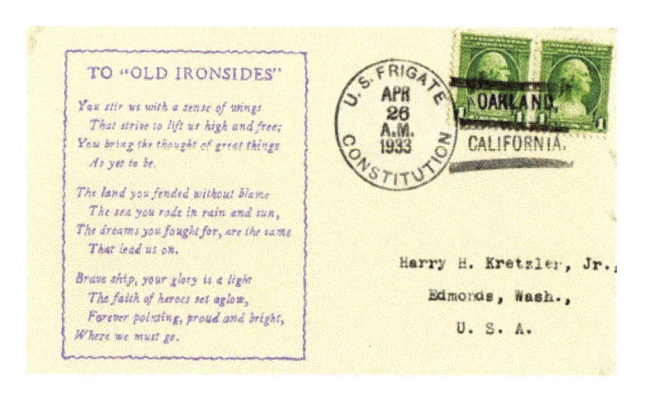

First Appearance E25 April 26

VALLEJO, CALIFORNIA: April 26, 1933 – May 2, 1933
Also at this port: S1, S5, E10a, E11
KILLER BARS: VALLEJO
                CALIFORNIA

OFFICIAL: Cachet sponsor North Bay Stamp Club & Vallejo Chamber of Commerce
First Appearance April 26 (3,000 covers)

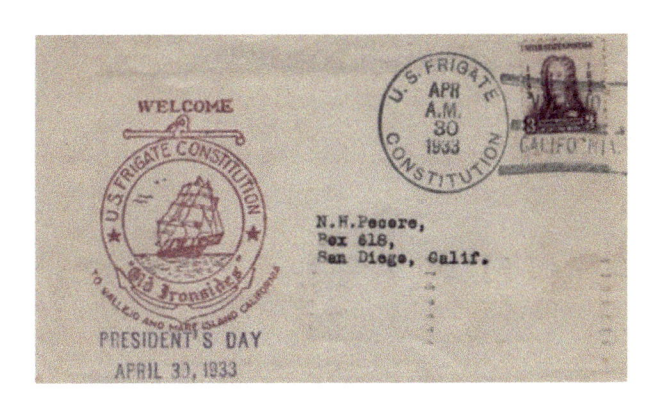

OFFICIAL: Cachet sponsor North Bay Stamp Club & Vallejo Chamber of Commerce
First Appearance April 30

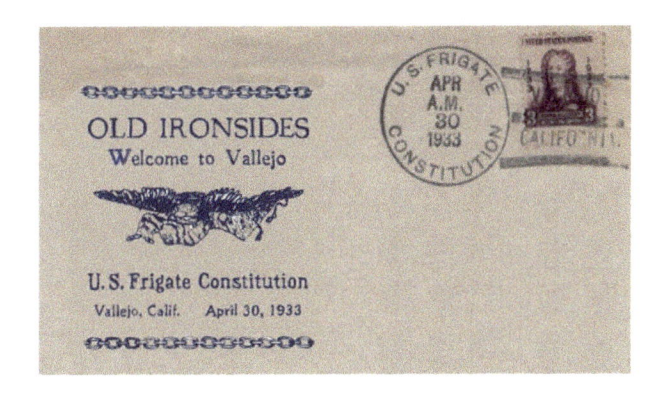

PRIVATE: Cachet sponsor Edward Hacker
First Appearance April 30

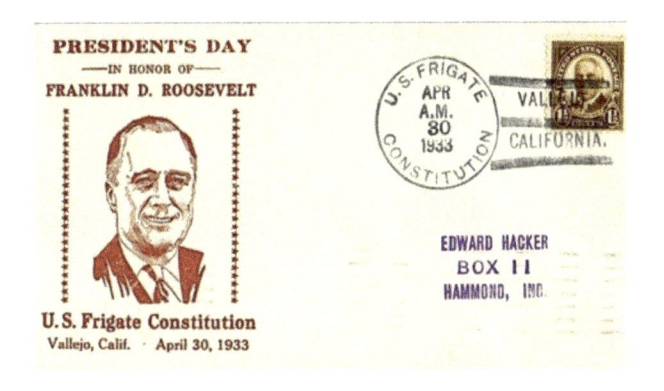

PRIVATE: Cachet sponsor unknown
First Appearance April 30

ENROUTE TO ASTORIA, OREGON: May 4, 1933
KILLER BARS: LAT. 41-16 N
 LONG. 124-12 W

ASTORIA, OREGON: May 6, 1933 – May 15, 1933
Also at this port: S2, S3, S5, E9, E10a
KILLER BARS: ASTORIA
 OREGON

OFFICIAL: Cachet sponsor Chamber of Commerce
First Appearance May 6 (3,743 covers)

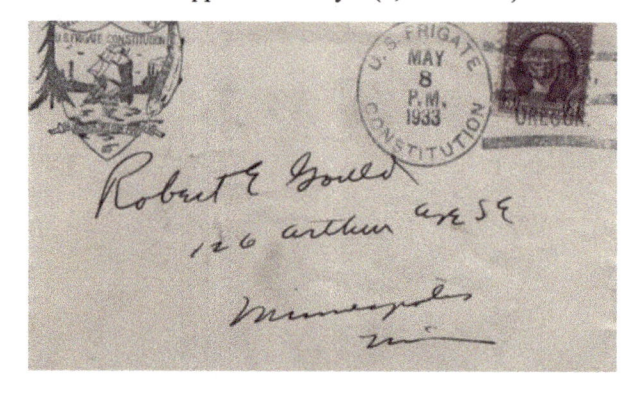

OFFICIAL: Cachet sponsor Chamber of Commerce
First Appearance May 6

PRIVATE: Cachet sponsor Dr. H. H. Kretzler
First Appearance May 13

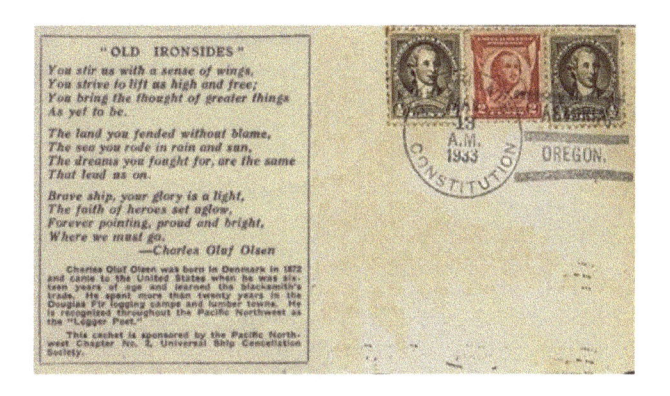

First Appearance Envelope Cachet E26 May 13

OFFICIAL: Cachet sponsor Chamber of Commerce
First Appearance May 14

OFFICIAL: Cachet sponsor Chamber of Commerce
First Appearance May 14

GRAYS HARBOR, WASHINGTON: May 16, 1933 – May 26, 1933
Also at this port: S1, S2, S3, E9, E10a, E26
KILLER BARS: GRAY'S
   HARBOR, WN

OFFICIAL: Cachet sponsor Grays Harbor Chamber of Commerce
First Appearance May 16 (15,000 covers)

Olympia "Oyster" money

PORT ANGELES, WASHINGTON: May 27, 1933 – May 31, 1933
Also at this port: S1, S2, S3, S4, S5, E10a, E11, E26
**KILLER BARS: PORT
                        ANGELES, WN**

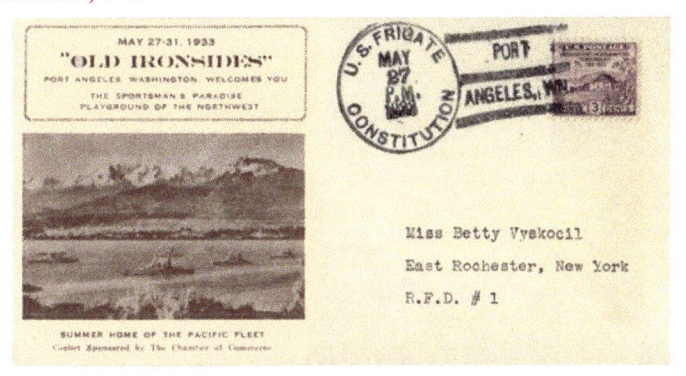

OFFICIAL: Cachet sponsor Chamber of Commerce
First Appearance May 27

OFFICIAL: Cachet sponsor Chamber of Commerce
First Appearance May 27

First Appearance E10c May 30

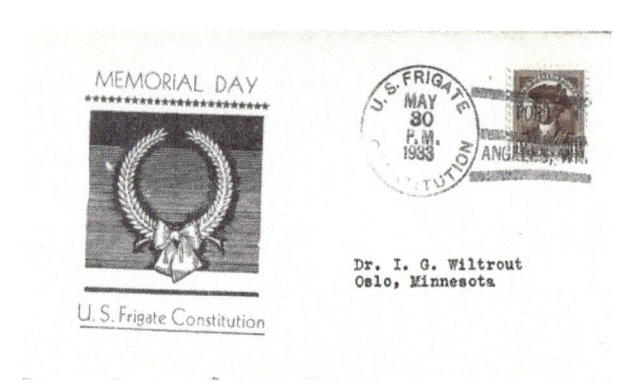

PRIVATE: Cachet sponsor John E. Gill
First Appearance May 30

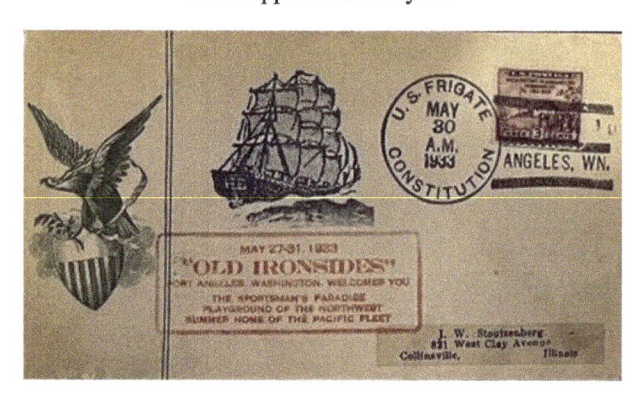

PRIVATE: Cachet sponsor unknown
First Appearance May 30

SEATTLE, WASHINGTON: May 31, 1933 – June 15, 1933
Also at this port: S1, S2, S3, E7, E9, E10a, E11, E12, E13, E18, E22, E21, E25, E26
KILLER BARS: SEATTLE
　　　　　　　　WASHINGTON

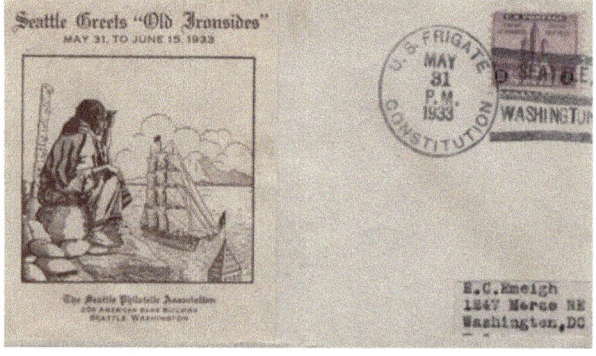

OFFICIAL: Cachet sponsor Seattle Philatelic Assoc.
First Appearance May 31 (900 covers)

84

OFFICIAL: Cachet sponsor Washington State Philatelic Society
First Appearance May 31 (25,622 covers - all dates)

OFFICIAL: Cachet sponsor American Legion Posts, Seattle
First Appearance June 3 (325 covers)

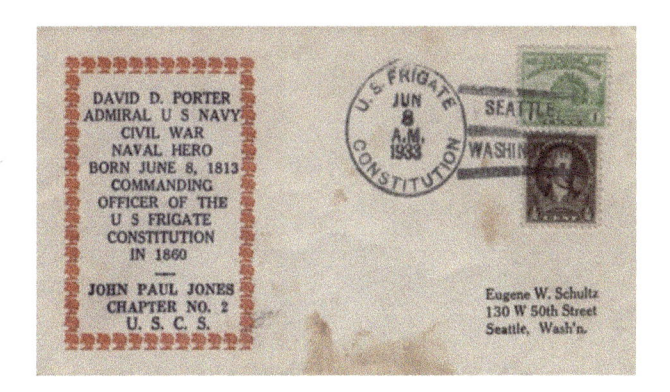

PRIVATE: Cachet sponsor John Paul Jones Chapter No. 2 USCS
First Appearance June 8 (44 covers)

OFFICIAL: Cachet sponsor John Paul Jones Chapter No. 2 USCS
First Appearance June 14

OFFICIAL: Cachet sponsor Washington State Philatelic Society
First Appearance June 14

OFFICIAL: Cachet sponsor Seattle Stamp Society
First Appearance June 14 (100 covers)
Used as place holder at Stamp Society Banquet

The 3 Flag Cachets of Seattle
Sponsored by John Paul Jones Chapter No. 2 USCS
Cachet Director D. C. Bartley

Hand Stamped (1987 covers)

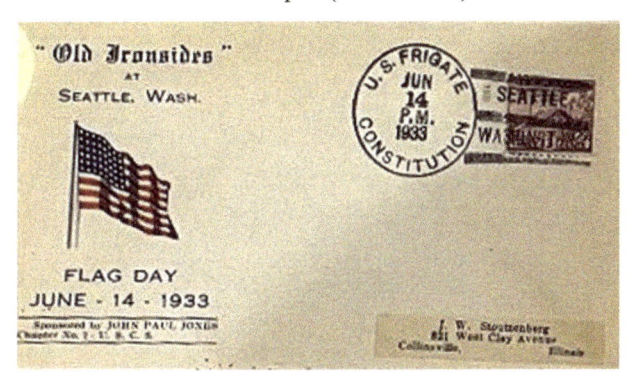

Printed (967 covers)

Gold Color 100 covers)

PRIVATE: Cachet sponsor Patriotic Order Sons of America, Pennsylvania State Camp
First Appearance June 14

PRIVATE: Cachet sponsor unknown
First Appearance June 14

PRIVATE: Cachet sponsor Seattle Stamp Society
First Appearance June 14

PRIVATE: Cachet sponsor unknown
First Appearance June 14

PRIVATE: Cachet sponsor unknown
First Appearance June 15

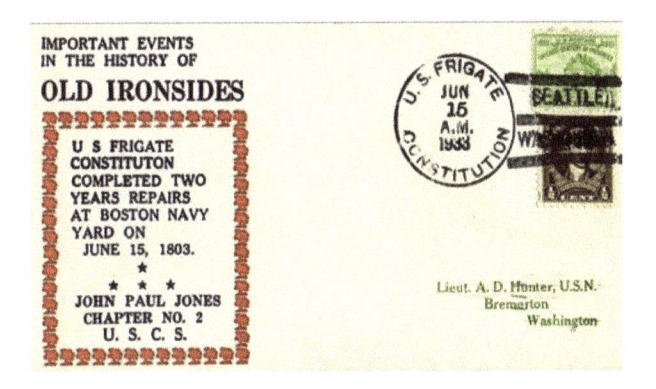

PRIVATE: Cachet sponsor John Paul Jones Chapter No. 2 USCS
First Appearance June 15 (44 covers)

PRIVATE: Cachet sponsor John Paul Jones Chapter No. 2 USCS
First Appearance June 15 (57 covers)

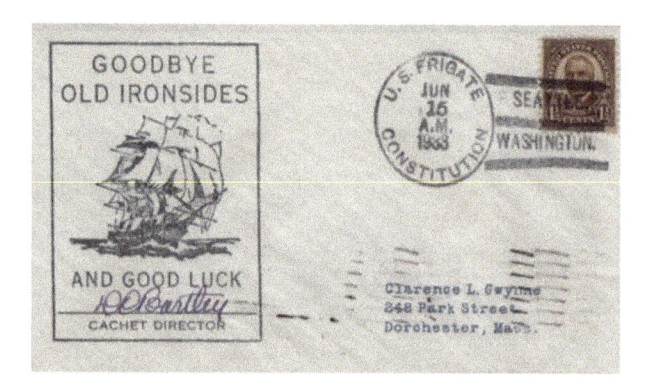

OFFICIAL: Cachet sponsor D.C. Bartley
First Appearance June 15 (1,713 covers)

TACOMA, WASHINGTON: June 15, 1933 – June 22, 1933
Also at this port: S1, S2, S3, E9, E10a, E11, E26
KILLER BARS: TACOMA
　　　　　　　　WASHINGTON

OFFICIAL: Cachet sponsor Chamber of Commerce
First Appearance June 15 (450 covers)
Also Available with Blue and Black overprint

OFFICIAL: Cachet sponsor Chamber of Commerce
First Appearance June 16

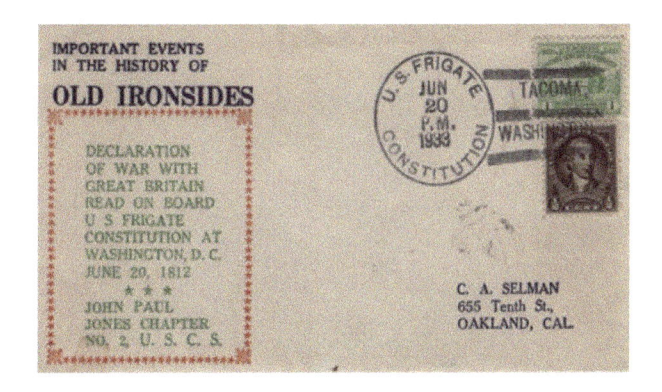

PRIVATE: Cachet sponsor John Paul Jones Chapter No. 2 USCS
First Appearance June 17

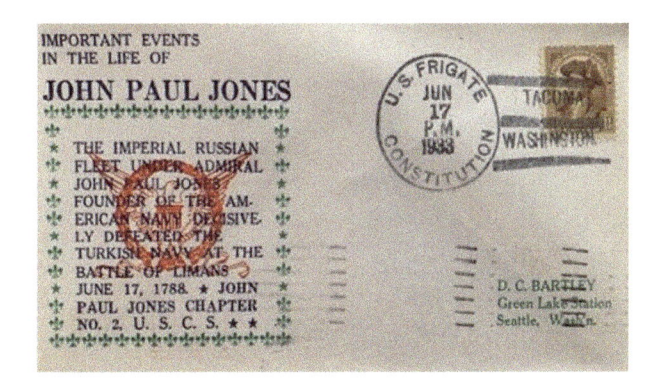

PRIVATE: Cachet sponsor John Paul Jones Chapter No. 2 USCS
First Appearance June 20

OLYMPIA, WASHINGTON: June 22, 1933 – July 1, 1933
Also at this port: S1, S2, S3, S4, S5, E2, E10a, E11, E26
KILLER BARS: OLYMPIA
                       WASHINGTON

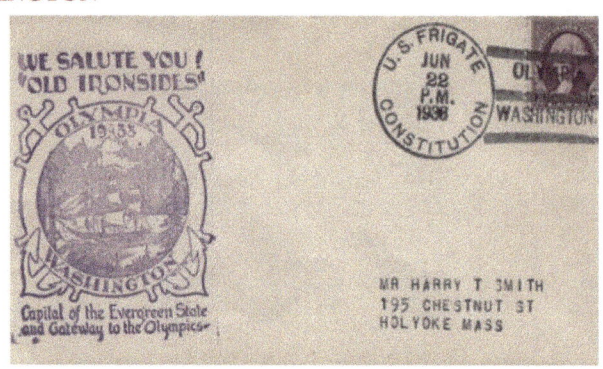

OFFICIAL: Cachet sponsor Chamber of Commerce
First Appearance June 22

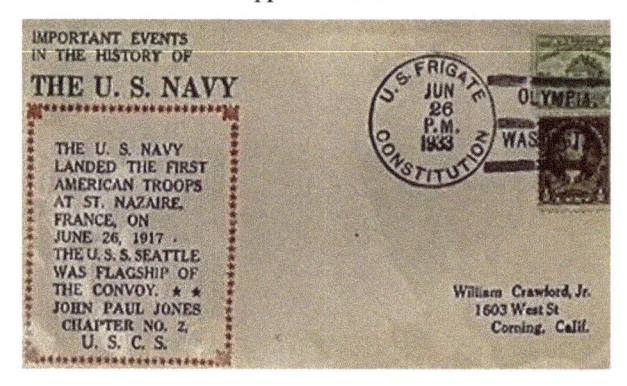

PRIVATE: Cachet sponsor John Paul Jones Chapter No. 2 USCS
First Appearance June 26

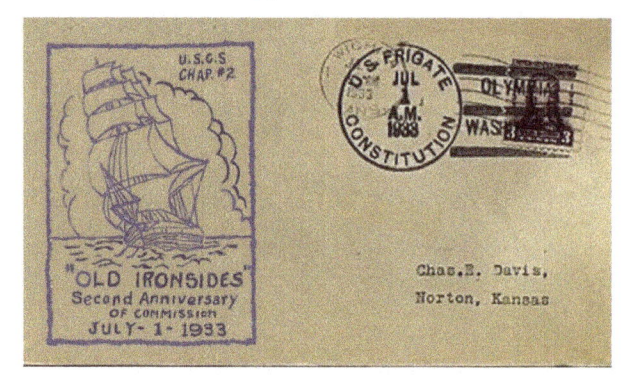

PRIVATE: Cachet sponsor John Paul Jones Chapter No. 2 USCS
First Appearance July 1 (50 covers)

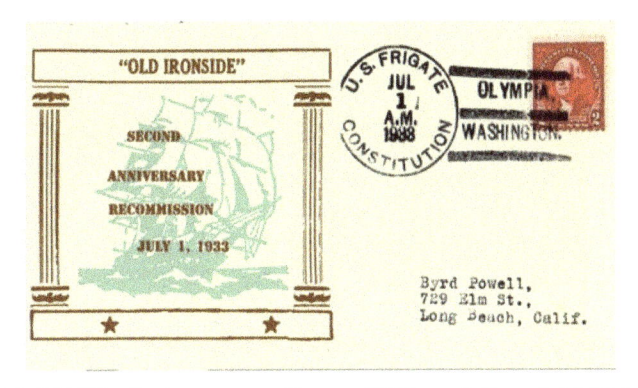

PRIVATE: Cachet sponsor Everett Wallster & Joseph M. Hale
First Appearance July 1

BREMERTON, WASHINGTON: July 1, 1933 – July 7, 1933
Also at this port: S!, S2, S3, S4, S5, E2, E9, E10a, E11, E12a, E13, E22, E23, E26
KILLER BARS: BREMERTON
WASHINGTON

OFFICIAL: Cachet sponsor San Pedro Chamber of Commerce
First Appearance July 1

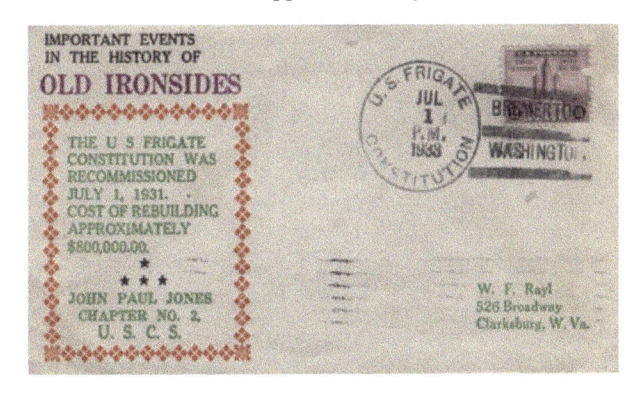

PRIVATE: Cachet sponsor John Paul Jones Chapter No. 2 USCS
First Appearance July 1 (111 covers)

92

PRIVATE: Cachet sponsor unknown
First Appearance July 4

PRIVATE: Cachet sponsor unknown
First Appearance July 4

Constitution at Bremerton, WA - July 4, 1933

OFFICIAL: Cachet sponsor John Paul Jones Chapter No. 2 USCS
First Appearance July 4 (2570 covers)

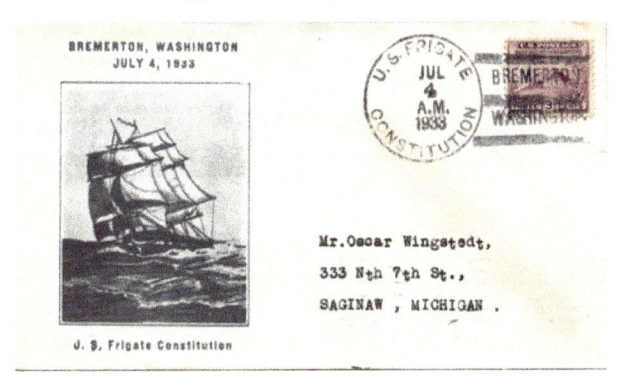

PRIVATE: Cachet sponsor Frank I. Morse
First Appearance July 4

EDMUNDS, WASHINGTON:
NOTE: On July 7, 1933 "Old Ironsides" on her way to Everett, Washington, passed close to the shores of Edmunds at 1:00 PM. As a special cachet had been printed for Edmunds, the covers were sent aboard the *Constitution* to be canceled. This was done with the approval of Commander Gulliver.
KILLER BARS: **EDMUNDS**
              WASHINGTON

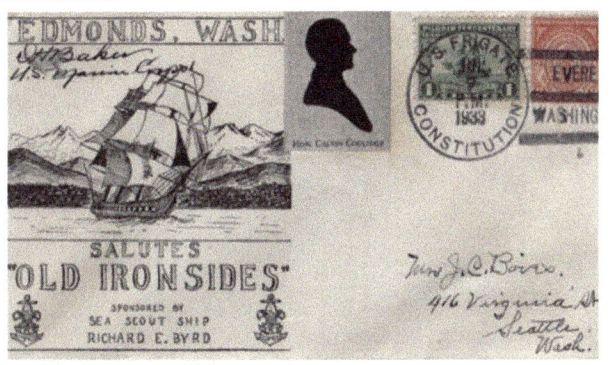

OFFICIAL: Cachet sponsor Sea Scout Ship "Richard E. Byrd"
First Appearance July 7

NOTE: On July 14, 1933 the *Constitution* on her way to Bellingham, again passed near Edmonds. The Sea Scout Ship came out to "Old Ironsides" and pick up from Quartermaster Stowe, 20 covers canceled the last day at Everett.

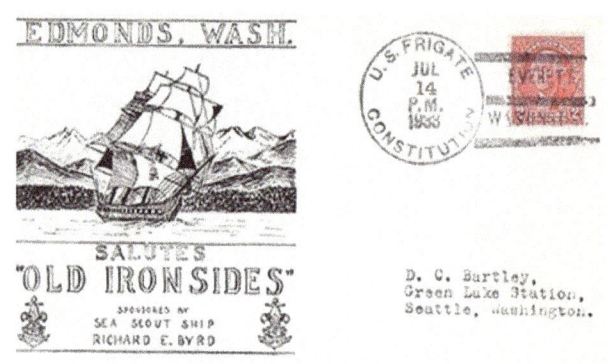

OFFICIAL: Sea Scout Ship "Richard E. Byrd"

EVERETT, WASHINGTON; July 7, 1933 – July 14, 1933
Also at this port: S1, S3, S5, E10a, E11, E26
KILLER BARS: EVERETT
                        WASHINGTON

OFFICIAL: Cachet sponsor Chamber of Commerce
First Appearance July 7

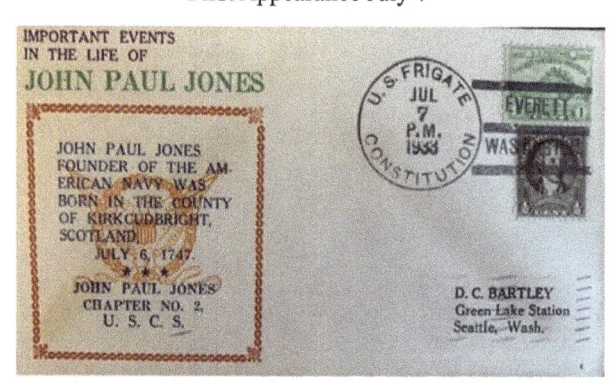

PRIVATE: Cachet sponsor John Paul Jones Chapter No. 2 USCS
First Appearance June 7

PRIVATE: Cachet sponsor Dr. H. H. Kretzler
First Appearance July 11 (100 cards)

BELLINGHAM, WASHINGTON; July 14, 1933 – July 20, 1933
Also at this port: S1, S2, S3, S4, S5, E2, E10a, E11, E21, E26
KILLER BARS: BELLINGHAM
WASHINGTON

OFFICIAL: Cachet sponsor Chamber of Commerce
First Appearance July 14

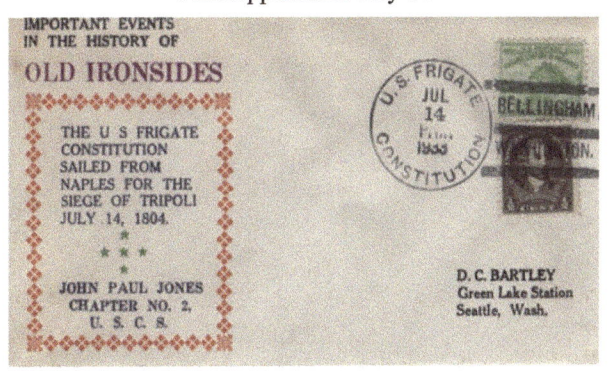

PRIVATE: Cachet sponsor John Paul Jones Chapter No. 2 USCS
First Appearance July 14

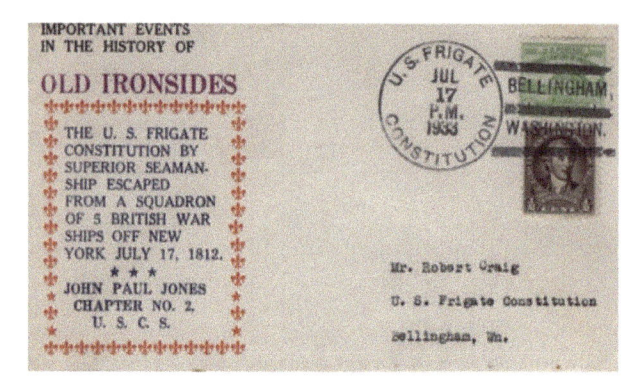

PRIVATE: Cachet sponsor John Paul Jones Chapter No. 2 USCS
First Appearance July 17 (82 covers)

PRIVATE: Cachet sponsor Dr. H. H. Kretzler
First Appearance July 17 (100 cards)

ANACORTES, WASHINGTON; July 20, 1933 – July 26, 1933
Also at this port: S1, S2, S3, S4, S5, E2, E10a, E11, E17, E18, E26
KILLER BARS: ANACORTES
                WASHINGTON

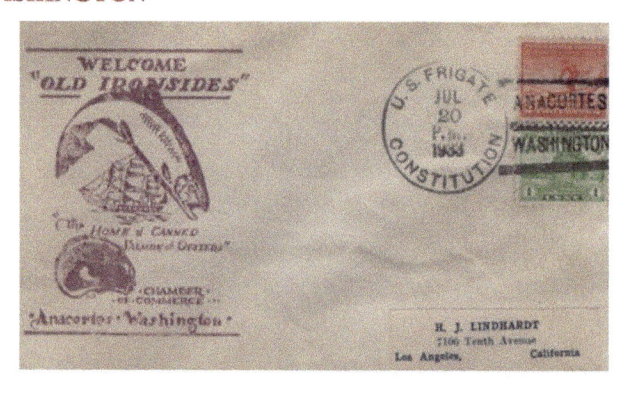

OFFICIAL: Cachet sponsor Chamber of Commerce
First Appearance July 20

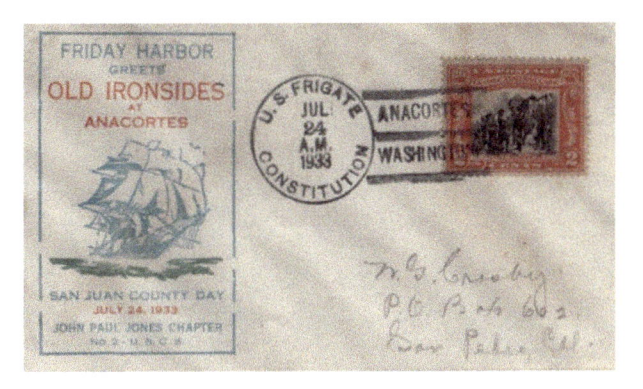

OFFICIAL: Cachet sponsor John Paul Jones Chapter No. 2 USCS

First Appearance July 24

NOTE: Friday Harbor was in the original itinerary of "Old Ironsides", but two weeks before the date of arrival, the port was canceled because of "dangerous Waters". Because there were over two thousand covers the decision was made to cancel these covers at Anacortes on July 24.

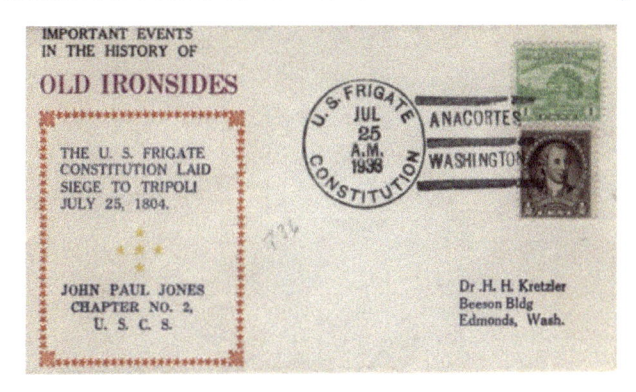

PRIVATE: Cachet sponsor John Paul Jones Chapter No. 2 USCS

First Appearance July 25

PORT TOWNSEND: July 26, 1933 – July 30, 1933
Also at this port: S1, S2, S3, S4, S5, E2, E10a, E11, E26
KILLER BARS: **PORT TOWN-**
                    SEND, WASH.

OFFICIAL: Cachet sponsor Chamber of Commerce

First Appearance July 26

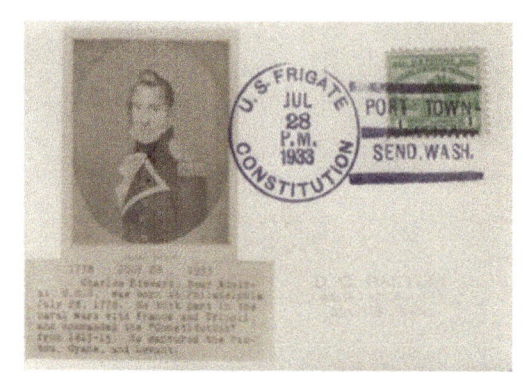

PRIVATE: Cachet sponsor Dr. H. H. Kretzler
First Appearance July 28 (100 cards)

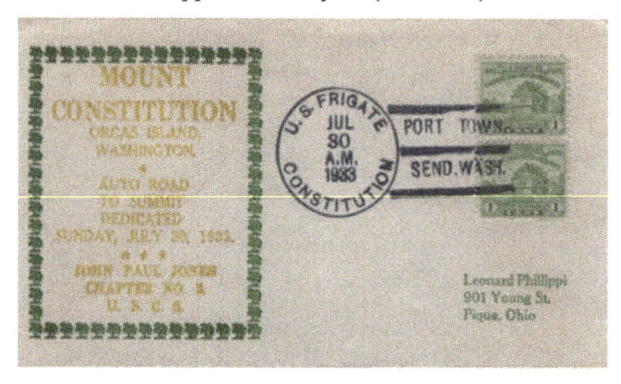

PRIVATE: Cachet sponsor John Paul Jones Chapter No. 2 USCS
First Appearance July 30 (110 covers)

ENROUTE TO PORTLAND, OREGON
Also at this port: S1, S2, S3, S4, S5
KILLER BARS: LAT 47-08 N.
                     LONG 124-36 W

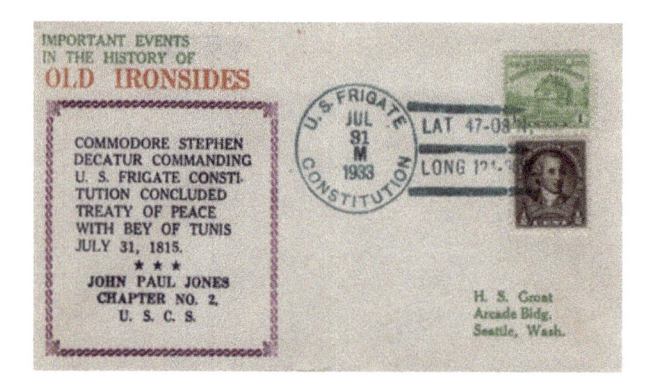

PRIVATE: Cachet sponsor John Paul Jones Chapter No. 2 USCS
First Appearance July 31 (144 covers)

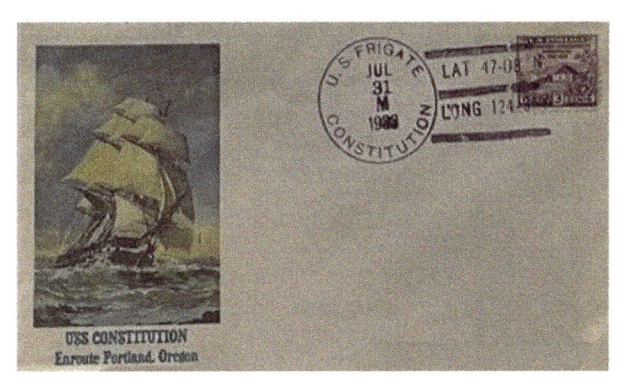

PRIVATE: Cachet sponsor unknown
First Appearance July 28

OFF TONGUE POINT OREGON
Also at this port: S1, S2, S3, S5, E10a
KILLER BARS: TONGUE PT
 ASTORIA, ORE

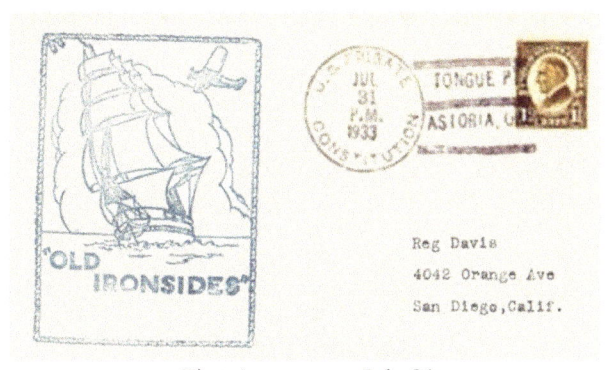

First Appearance July 31

PORTLAND, OREGON: August 2, 1933 – August 22, 1933
Also at this port: S1, E2, E9, E10a, E11, E14, E15, E 21, E26
KILLER BARS: PORTLAND
 OREGON

OFFICIAL: Cachet sponsor Oregon Stamp Society
First Appearance August 2

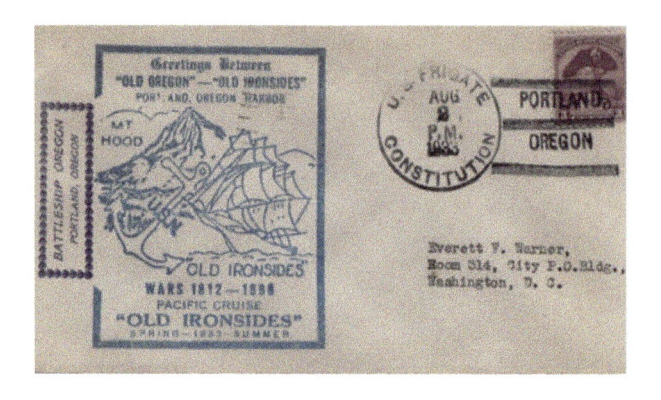

OFFICIAL: Cachet sponsor Edward E. Bryan
First Appearance August 2 (2725 covers)

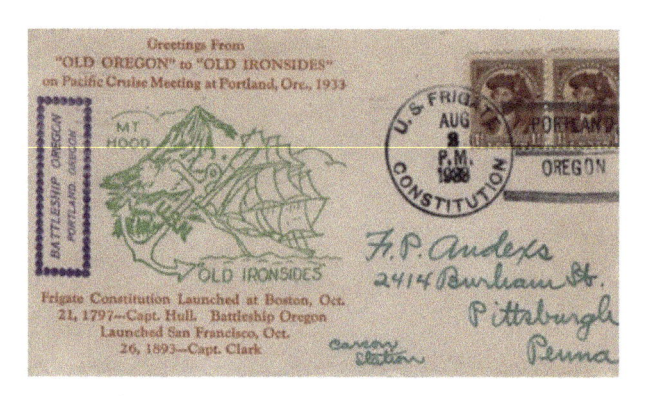

OFFICIAL: Cachet sponsor Edward E. Bryan
First Appearance August 2 (735 covers)

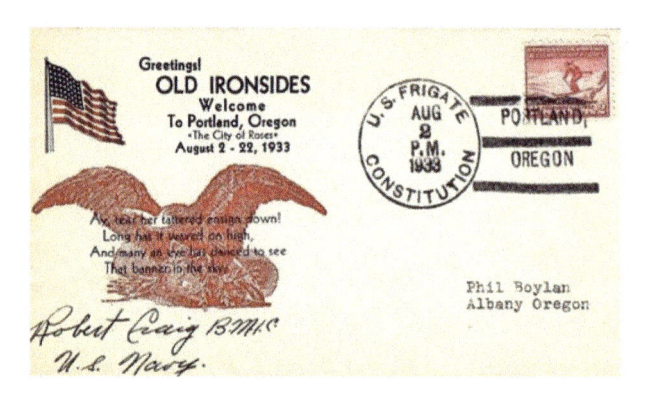

PRIVATE: Cachet sponsor unknown
First Appearance August 2

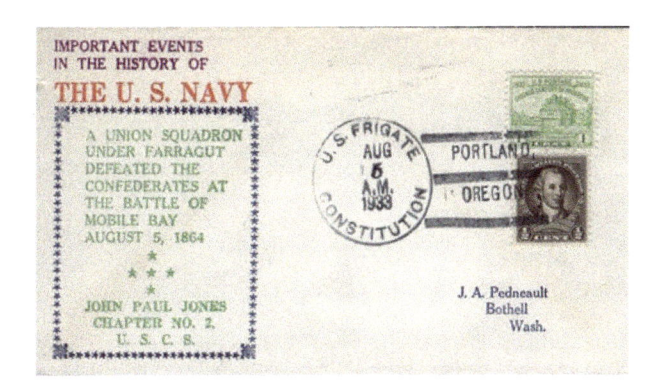

PRIVATE: Cachet sponsor John Paul Jones Chapter No. 2 USCS
First Appearance August 5

PRIVATE: Cachet sponsor John Paul Jones Chapter No. 2 USCS
First Appearance August 8

Presentation of Oregon State flag to Constitution crew

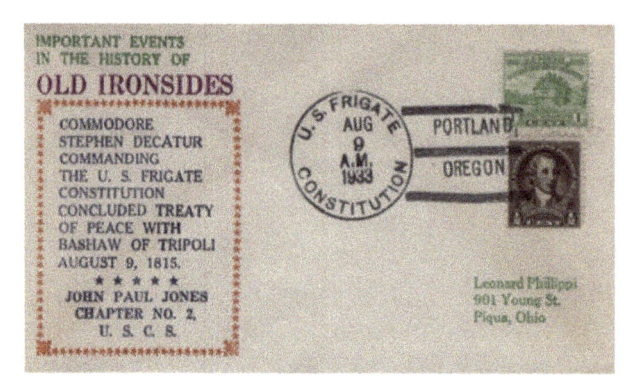

PRIVATE: Cachet sponsor John Paul Jones Chapter No. 2 USCS
First Appearance August 9 (95 covers)

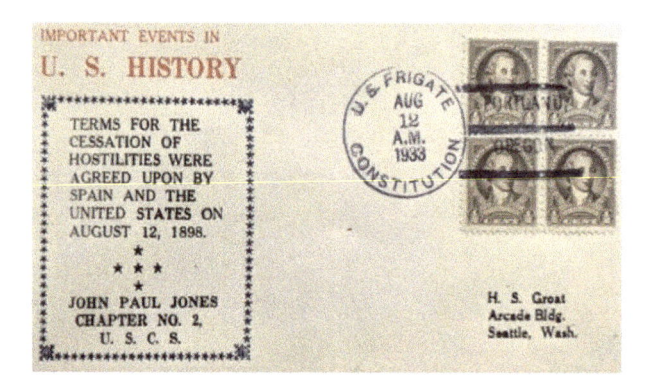

PRIVATE: Cachet sponsor John Paul Jones Chapter No. 2 USCS
First Appearance 12

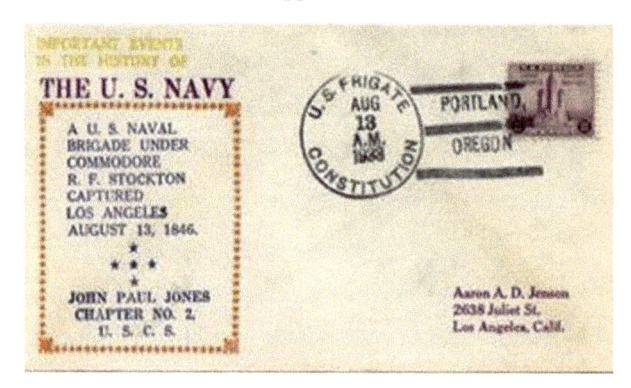

PRIVATE: Cachet sponsor John Paul Jones Chapter No. 2 USCS
First Appearance August 13

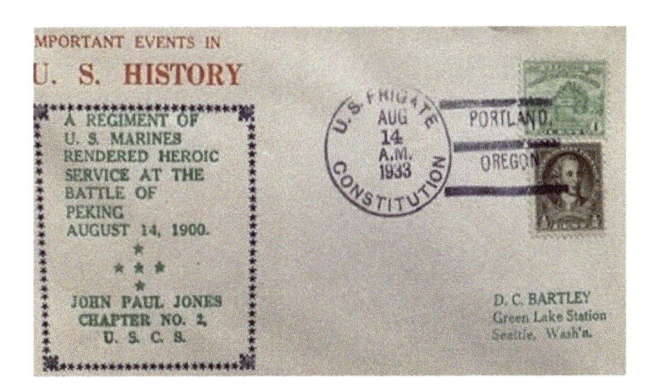

PRIVATE: Cachet sponsor John Paul Jones Chapter No. 2 USCS
First Appearance August 14

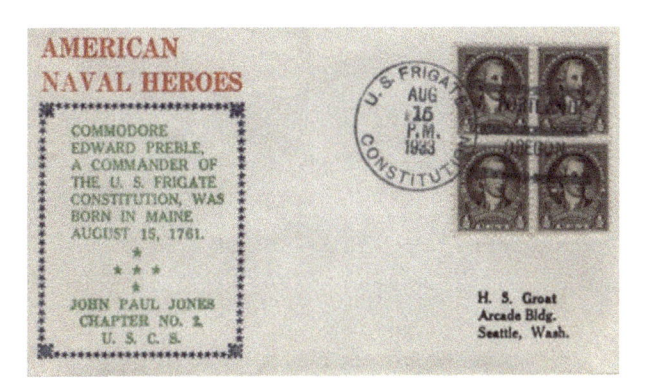

PRIVATE: Cachet sponsor John Paul Jones Chapter No. 2 USCS
First Appearance August 15 (70 covers)

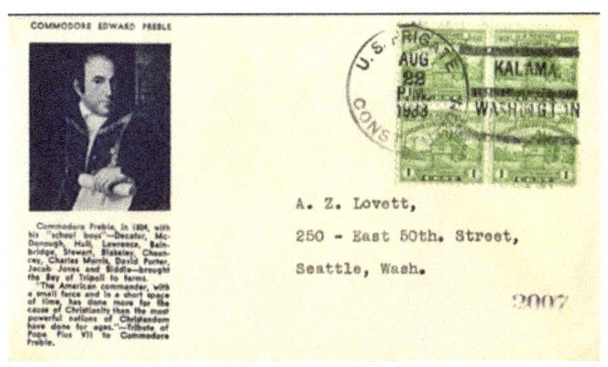

PRIVATE: Cachet sponsor Dr. H. H. Kretzler
First Appearance August 15 (100 cards)
NOTE: This cover is from Kalama, WA of a later date

PRIVATE: Cachet sponsor unknown
First Appearance August 19

PRIVATE: Cachet sponsor Dr. H. H. Kretzler
First Appearance August 19 (100 cards)

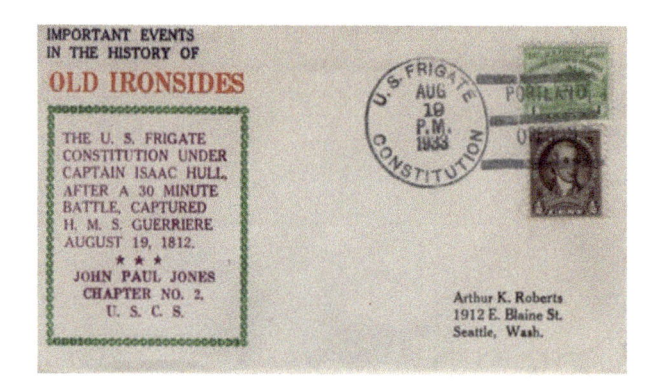

PRIVATE: Cachet sponsor John Paul Jones Chapter No. 2 USCS
First Appearance August 19 (132 covers)

PRIVATE: Cachet sponsor Joseph M. Hale & Everett Wallsster
First Appearance August 19 (200 covers)

PRIVATE: Cachet sponsor Edward Hacker
First Appearance August 19 (150 covers)

PRIVATE: Cachet sponsor John E. Gill
First Appearance August 19

PRIVATE: Cachet sponsor John E. Gill
First Appearance August 19

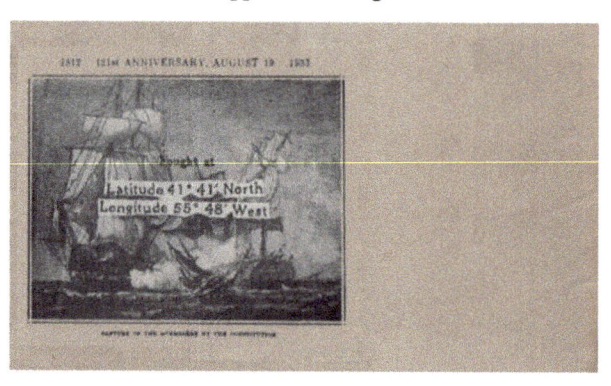

PRIVATE: Cachet sponsor John E. Gill
First Appearance August 19

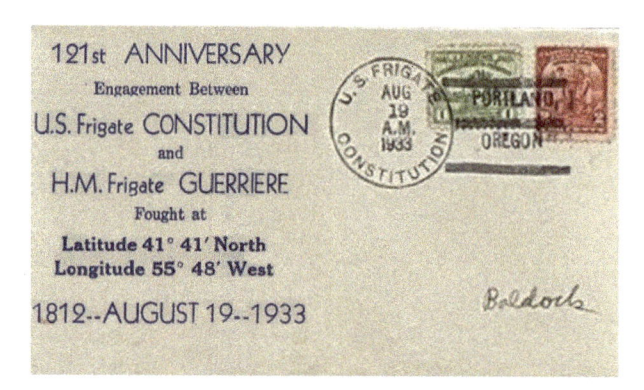

PRIVATE: Cachet sponsor John E. Gill
First Appearance August 19

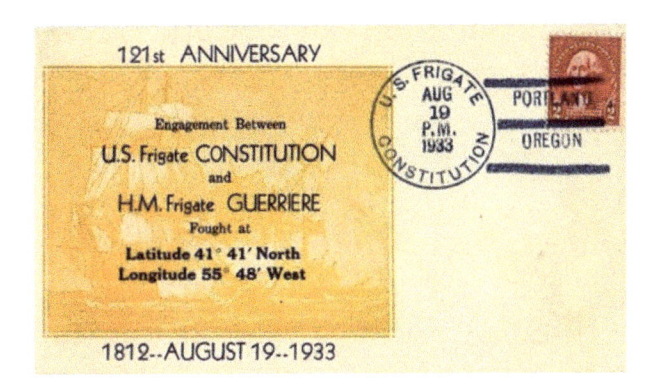

108

PRIVATE: Cachet sponsor John E. Gill
First Appearance August 19

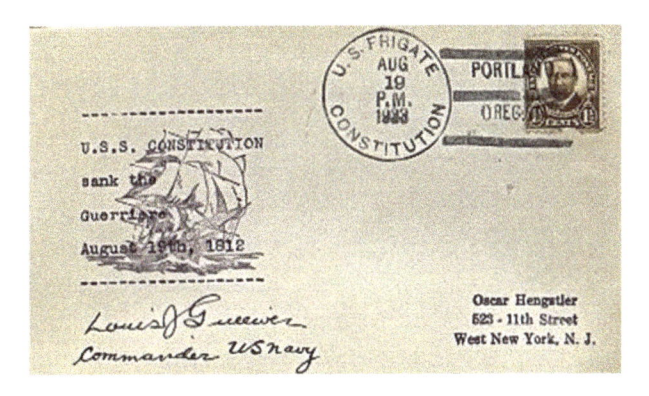

PRIVATE: Cachet sponsor unknown
First Appearance August 19

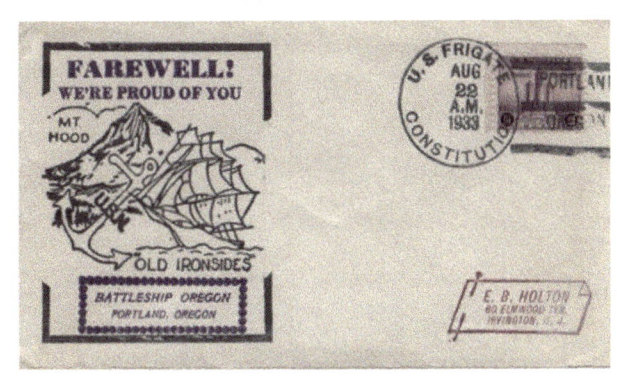

PRIVATE: Cachet sponsor Edward E. Bryan
First Appearance August 22

KALAMA, WASHINGTON; August 22, 1933 – August 24, 1933
Also at this port: S2, S4, S5, E2, E10a, E11, E26
KILLER BARS: KALAMA
　　　　　　　　WASHINGTON

OFFICIAL: Cachet sponsor Kalama Business Men's Club
First Appearance August 22 (6,722 covers)

LONGVIEW, WASHINGTON; August 24, 1933 August 28, 1933
Also at this port: S3, S5, E2, E9, E10a, E26
KILLER BARS: LONGVIEW
　　　　　　　　WASHINGTON

OFFICIAL: Cachet sponsor Chamber of Commerce
First Appearance August 24

Longview "wooden nickel"

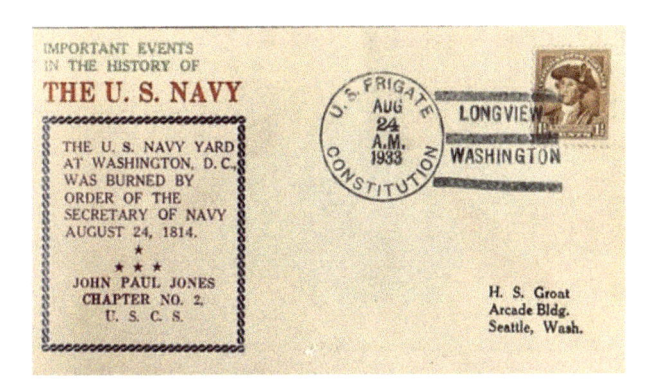

PRIVATE: Cachet sponsor John Paul Jones Chapter No. 2 USCS
First Appearance August 24

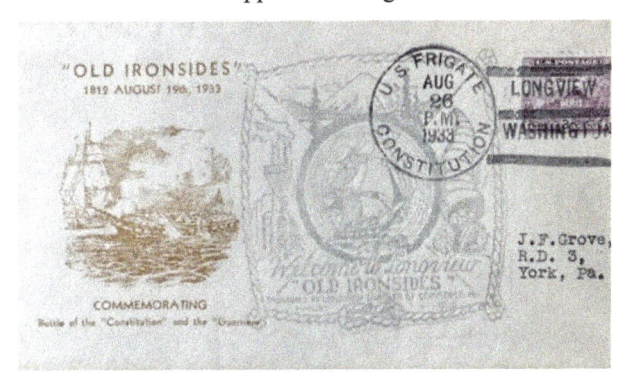

PRIVATE: Cachet sponsor unknown
First Appearance August 26

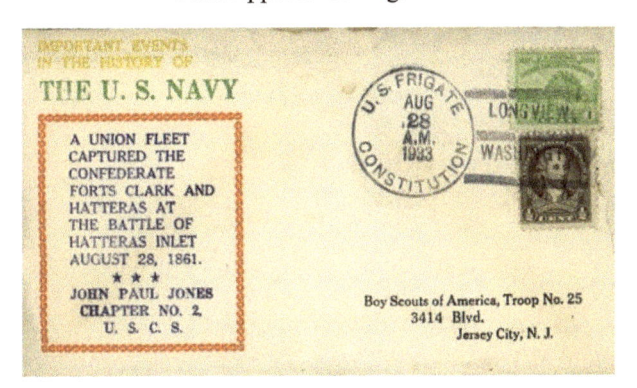

PRIVATE: Cachet sponsor John Paul Jones Chapter No. 2 USCS
First Appearance August 28

ENROUTE TO SAN FRANCISCO: August 29, 1933
Also at this port: S1, S2, E10a
KILLER BARS: OFF OREGON COAST

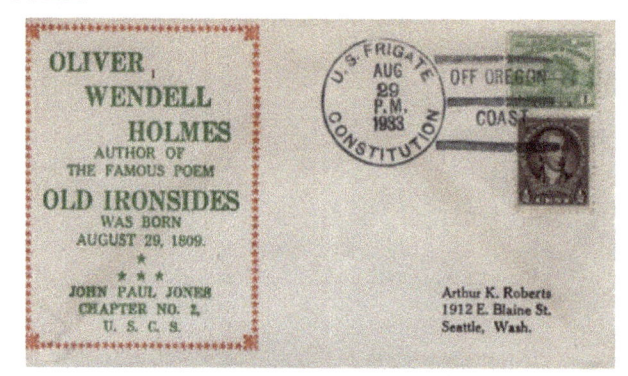

PRIVATE: Cachet sponsor John Paul Jones Chapter No. 2 USCS
First Appearance August 29

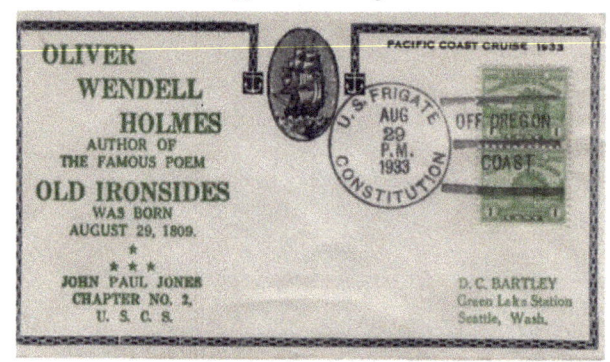

PRIVATE: Cachet sponsor John Paul Jones Chapter No. 2 USCS
First Appearance August 29

CRESCENT CITY, CALIFORNIA: August 30, 1933

NOTE: This Northern California city had a cachet prepared and covers cacheted in honor of the Frigate Constitution passing south bound along the coast. However, the cachet sponsor was unable to get aboard "Old Ironsides" as she passed by, so the covers were canceled in the local Post Office.

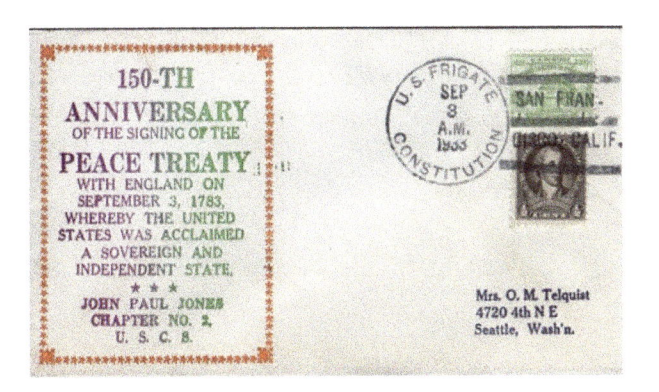

PRIVATE: Cachet sponsor John Paul Jones Chapter No. 2 USCS
First Appearance September 3

First Appearance of "Ship Cachet' S6 September 4

PRIVATE: Cachet sponsor John Paul Jones Chapter No. 2 USCS
First Appearance September 8 (108 covers)

SAN FRANCISCO, CALIFORNIA: August 31, 1933 – September 15, 1933
Also at this port: S1, S2, S3, S4, S5, E2, E10a, E11
KILLER BARS: SAN FRAN-
               CISCO CALIF.

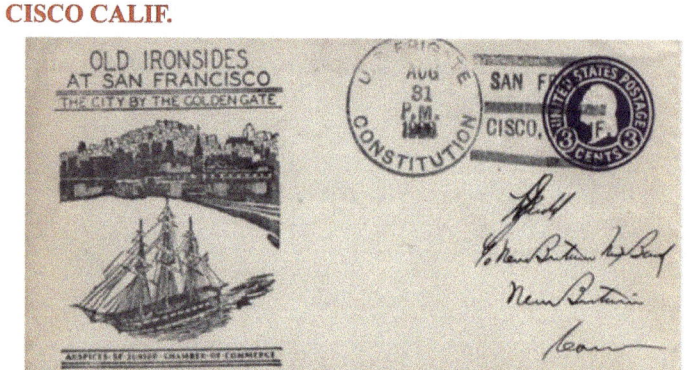

OFFICIAL: Cachet Sponsor San Francisco Junior Chamber of Commerce
First Appearance August 31 (2550 covers)

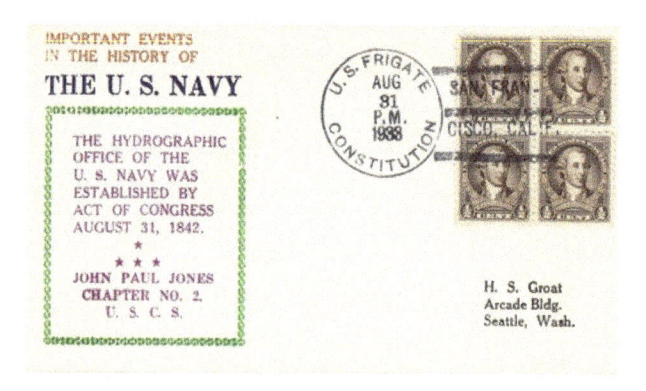

PRIVATE: Cachet sponsor John Paul Jones Chapter No. 2 USCS
First Appearance August 31

PRIVATE: Cachet sponsor John Paul Jones Chapter No. 2 USCS
First Appearance September 2

PRIVATE: Cachet sponsor John Paul Jones Chapter No. 2 USCS
First Appearance September 8

OFFICIAL: Cachet sponsor unknown
First Appearance September 10 (350 covers)

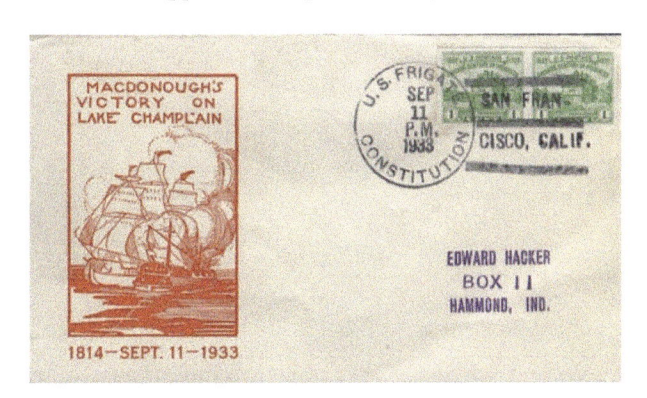

OFFICIAL: Cachet sponsor unknown
First Appearance September 10 (350 covers)

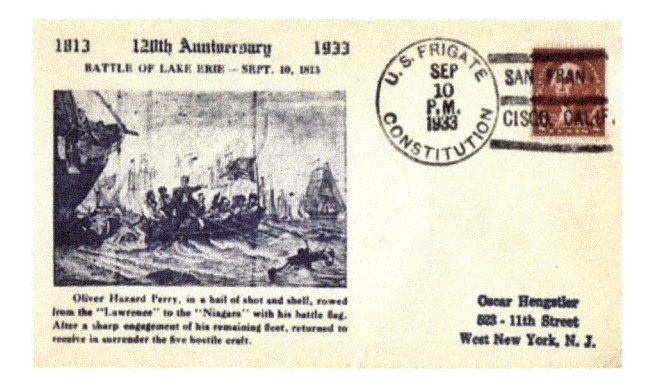

PRIVATE: Cachet sponsor unknown
First Appearance September 10

Constitution moored at Market St. Pier, Oakland, CA

OAKLAND, CALIFORNIA: September 15, 1933 – September 29, 1933
Also at this port: S1, S2, S3, S4, S5, S6, E10a,
KILLER BARS: OAKLAND
    CALIF.

OFFICIAL: Cachet sponsor The Aiglon Club
First Appearance September 15 (3418 covers)

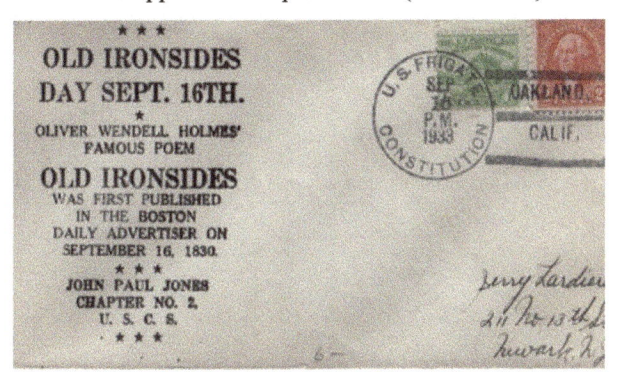

PRIVATE: Cachet sponsor John Paul Jones Chapter No. 2 USCS
First Appearance September 16 (1411 covers)

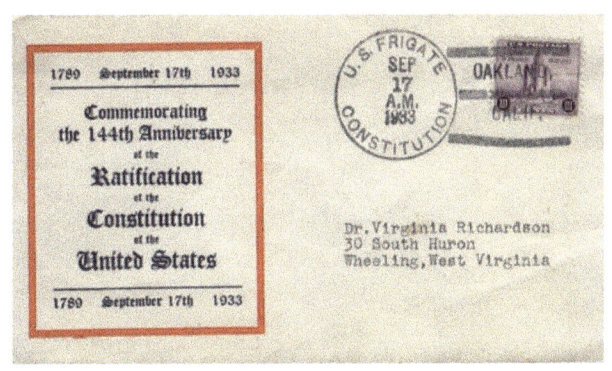

PRIVATE: Cachet sponsor unknown
First Appearance September 17

116

OFFICIAL: Cachet sponsor The Aiglon Club
First Appearance September 17 (2705 covers)

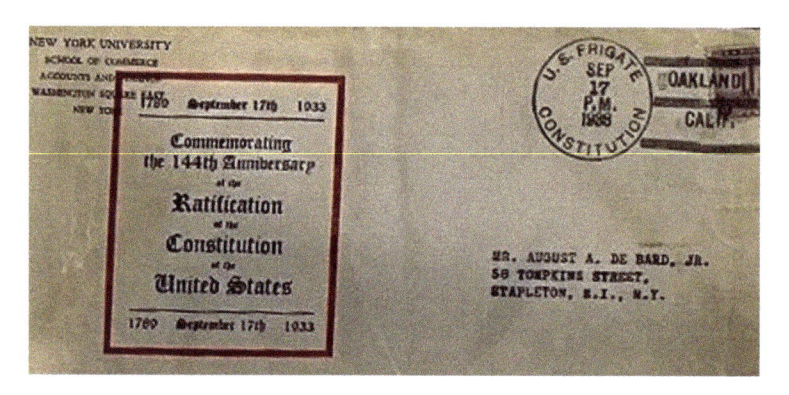

PRIVATE: Cachet sponsor unknown
First Appearance September 17

PRIVATE: Cachet sponsor John Paul Jones Chapter No. 2 USCS
First Appearance September 17

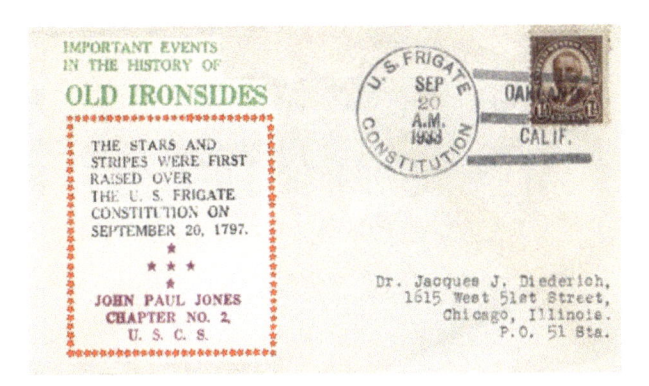

PRIVATE: Cachet sponsor John Paul Jones Chapter No. 2 USCS
First Appearance September 20 (130 covers)

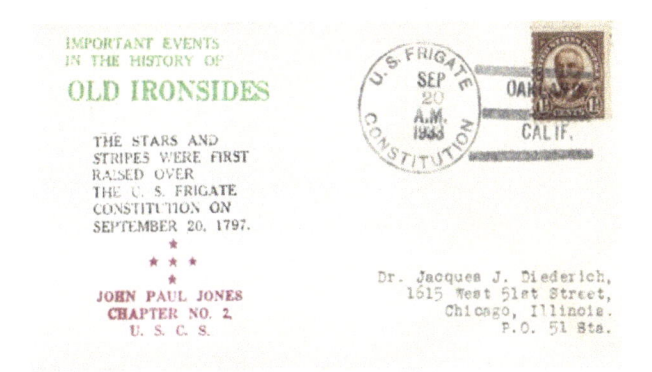

PRIVATE: Cachet sponsor John Paul Jones Chapter No. 2 USCS
First Appearance September 20

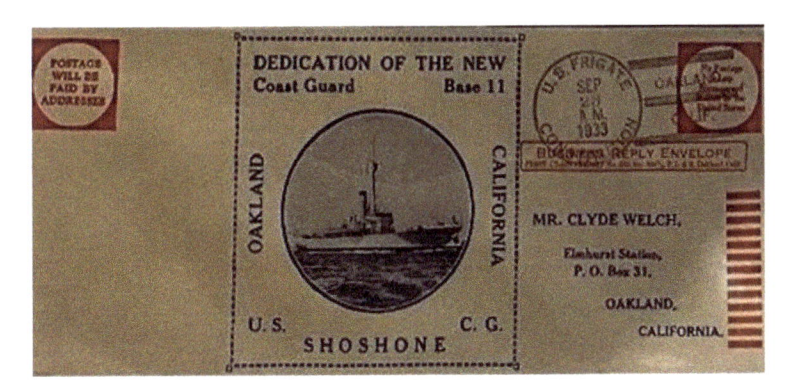

PRIVATE: Cachet sponsor unknown
First Appearance September 23

118

PRIVATE: Cachet sponsor Aiglon Club
First Appearance September 23

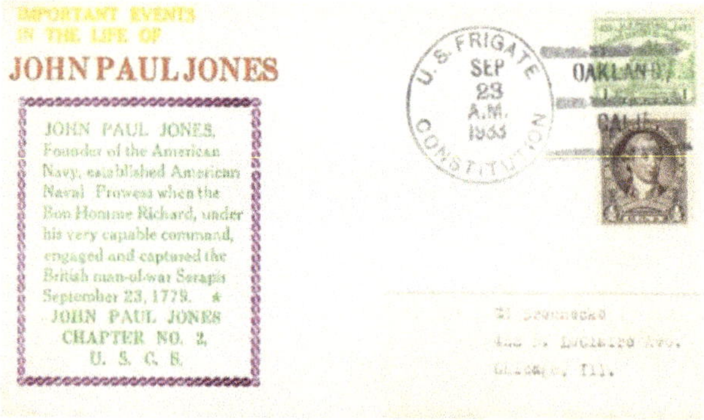

PRIVATE: Cachet sponsor John Paul Jones Chapter No. 2 USCS
First Appearance September 23

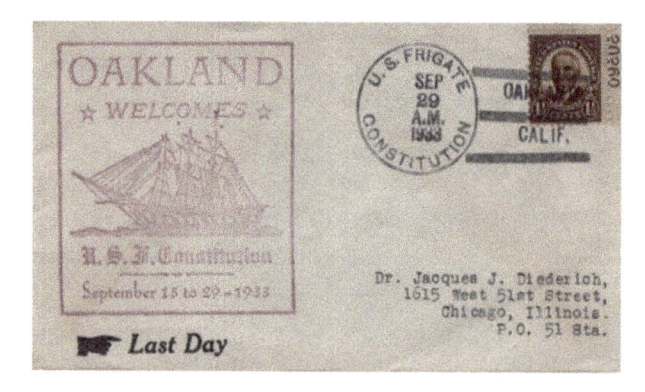

OFFICIAL: Cachet sponsor Aiglon Club
First Appearance September 29 (3500 covers)

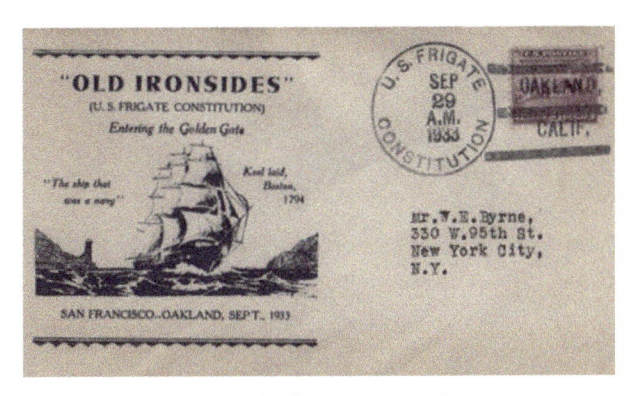

PRIVATE: Cachet sponsor unknown
First Appearance September 29

SANTA CRUZ, CALIFORNIA: September 29, 1933 – September 30, 1933
Also at this port: S3, S4, E2, E10a,
KILLER BARS: SANTA CRUZ
HARBOR

OFFICIAL: Cachet sponsor Chamber of Commerce
First Appearance September 30 (7607 covers)

Constitution anchored 1/2 mile out in harbor

MONTEREY, CALIFORNIA: September 30, 1933 – OCTOBER 1, 1933
Also at this port: S1, S6, E2, E10a, E11
KILLER BARS: MONTEREY
HARBOR

OFFICIAL: Cachet sponsor Chamber of Commerce
First Appearance October 1 (1500 covers)

PORT SAN LOUIS, CALIFORNIA: October 2,
NOTE: Attempted to enter Port of San Luis, but due to fog abandoned attempts and proceeded to Santa Barbara
Also at this port: S6, E10a, E11
KILLER BARS: OFF PORT
SAN LUIS

OFFICIAL: Cachet sponsor San Luis Obispo Chamber of Commerce
First Appearance October 2 (2000 covers)

OFFICIAL: Cachet sponsor Santa Maria Chamber of Commerce
First Appearance October 2 (2954 covers)

SANTA BARBARA, CALIFORNIA: October 3, 1933 – October 4, 1933
Also at this port: S6, E10a, E11
KILLER BARS: SANTA BARBARA
               HARBOR

OFFICIAL: Cachet sponsor Chamber of Commerce
First Appearance October 3 (2000 covers)

VENTURA, CALIFORNIA: October 4, 1933 – October 5, 1933
Also at this port: S1, S3, S4, S5, S6, E2, E10a, E11
KILLER BARS: VENTURA
                    HARBOR

PRIVATE: Cachet sponsor Chamber of Commerce
First Appearance October 4 (1000 covers)

SANTA MONICA, CALIFORNIA; October 5, 1933
Also at this port: S6
KILLER BARS: SANTA MONICA
                    HARBOR

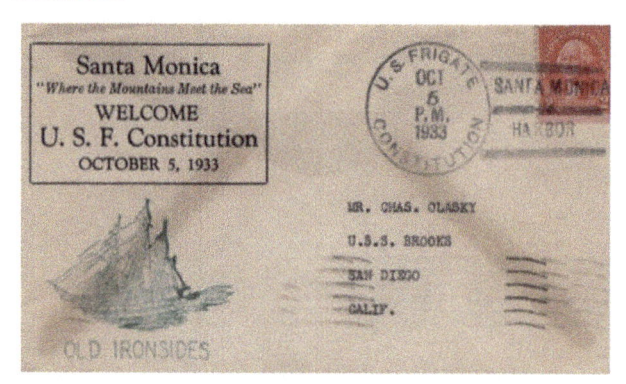

OFFICIAL: Cachet sponsor Lee H. Young
First Appearance October 5 (315 covers)

LONG BEACH, CALIFORNIA: October 6, 1933 – October 19, 1933
Also at this port: S1, S3, S4, S5, S6, E2, E9, E10a, E11
KILLER BARS: LONG BEACH
                           CALIF.

OFFICIAL: Cachet sponsor Chamber of Commerce
First Appearance October 6 (7301 covers)

PRIVATE: Cachet sponsor Byrd. L. Powell
First Appearance October 12 (1365 covers)

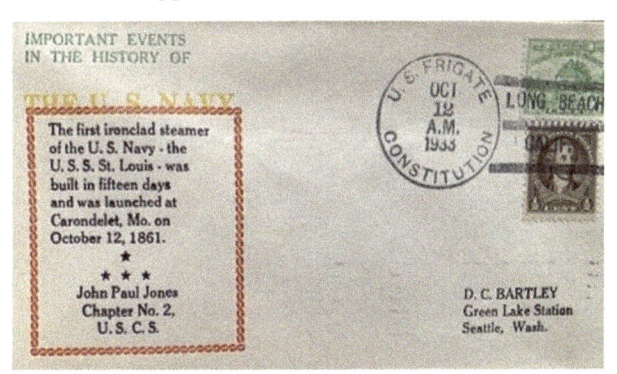

PRIVATE: Cachet sponsor John Paul Jones Chapter No. 2 USCS
First Appearance October 12

124

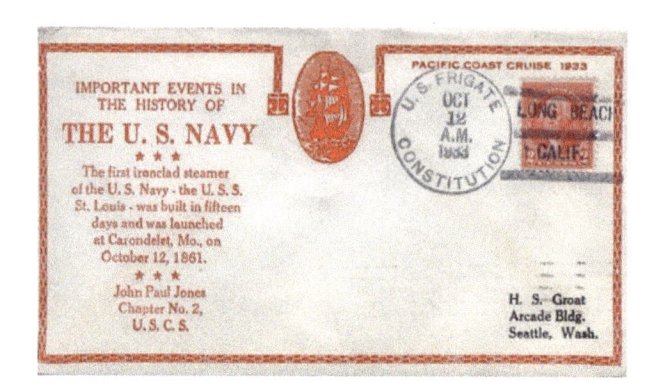

PRIVATE: Cachet sponsor John Paul Jones Chapter No. 2 USCS
First Appearance October 12

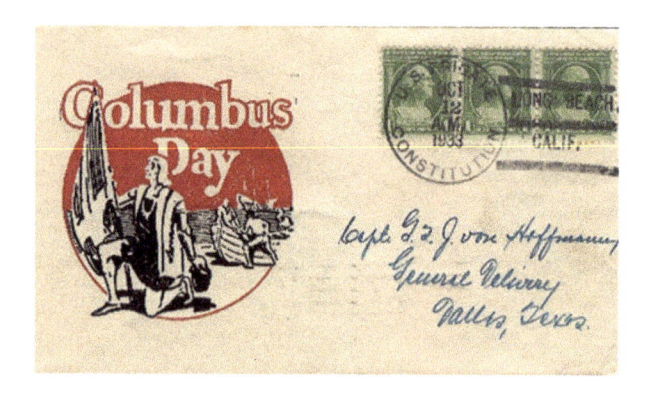

PRIVATE: Cachet sponsor unknown
First Appearance October 12

Constitution moored to Pier 1, Inner Harbor, Long Beach, CA

OFFICIAL: Cachet sponsor Byrd L. Powell
First Appearance October 12

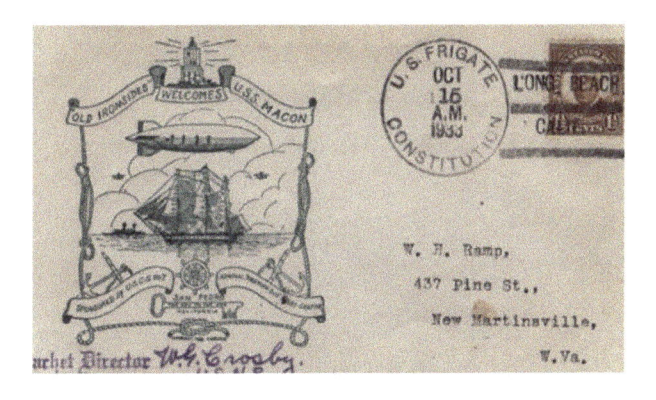

OFFICIAL: Cachet sponsor Fighting Bob Evans Chapter 7 USCS
First Appearance October 15 (1519 covers)

OFFICIAL: Cachet sponsor Chamber of Commerce
First Appearance October 15 (744 covers)

SAN PEDRO, CALIFORNIA: October 19, 1933 – November 2, 1933
Also at this port: S1, S2, S3, S4, S5, S6, E2, E10a, E11, E12
KILLER BARS: SAN PEDRO
                CALIF.

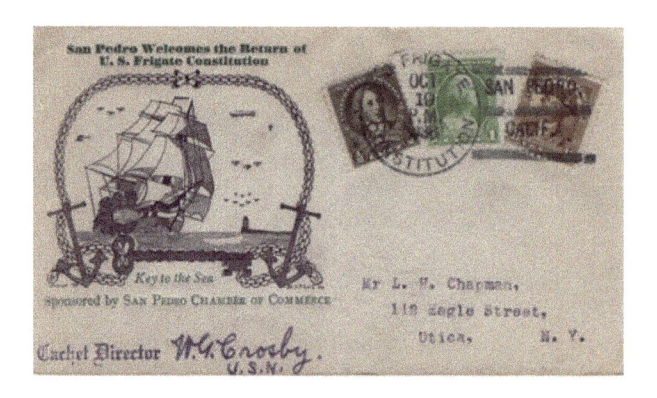

OFFICIAL: Cachet sponsor Chamber of Commerce
First Appearance October 19 (3650 covers)

First appearance 'Ship Cachets' S7 October 19

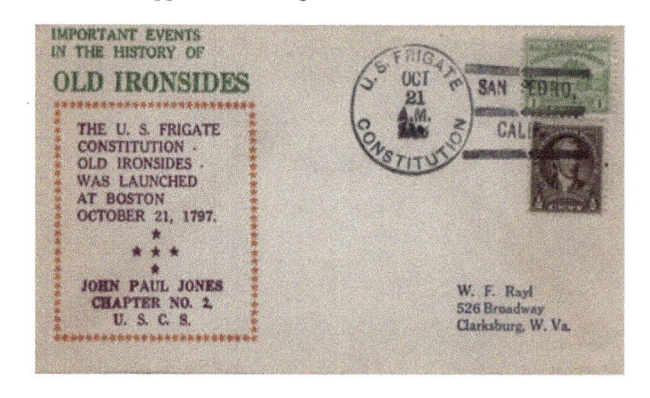

PRIVATE: Cachet sponsor John Paul Jones Chapter No. 2 USCS
First Appearance October 21 (85 covers)

PRIVATE: Cachet sponsor Joseph M Hale & Everett Wallster
First Appearance October 21

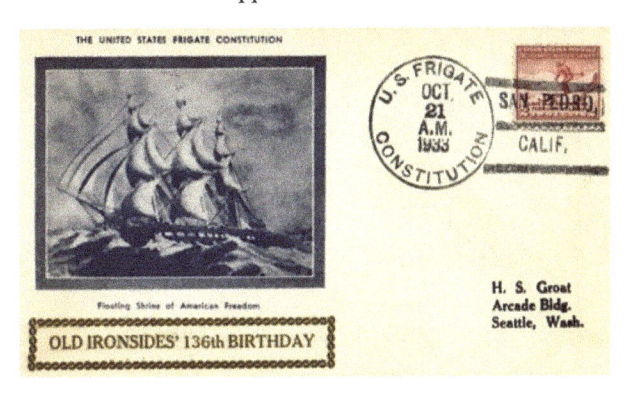

OFFICIAL: Cachet sponsor unknown
First Appearance October 21

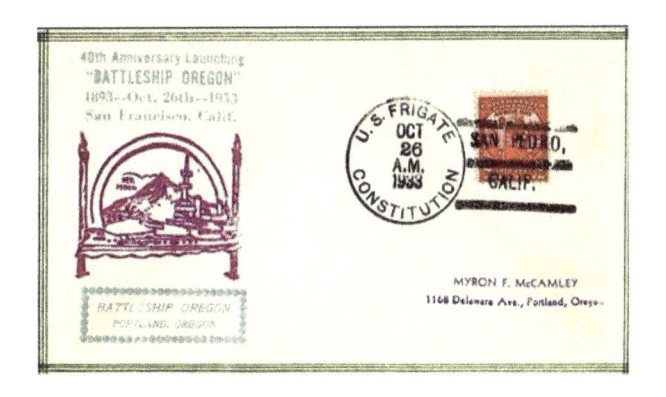

PRIVATE: Cachet sponsor Myron F. McCamley
First Appearance October 26

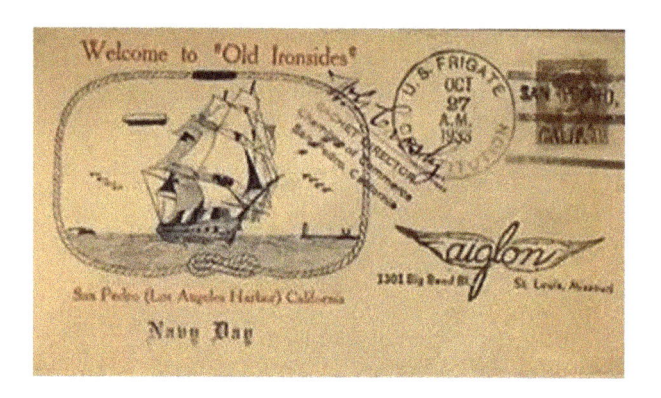

OFFICIAL: Cachet sponsor San Pedro Chamber of Commerce
First Appearance October 27 (103 covers)

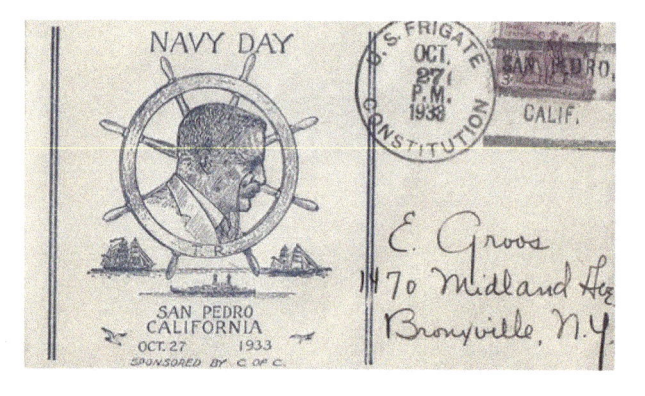

OFFICIAL: Cachet sponsor San Pedro Chamber of Commerce
First Appearance October 27 (5316 covers)

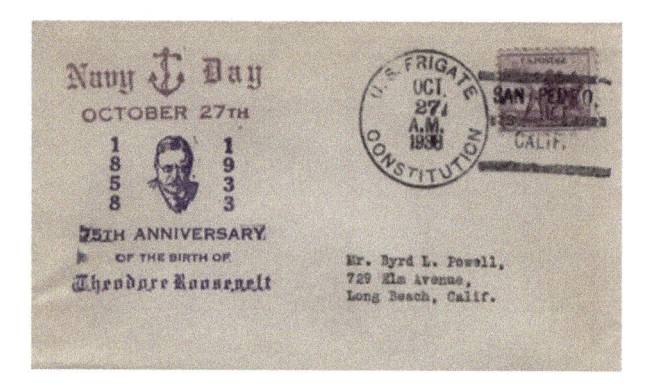

OFFICIAL: Cachet sponsor Byrd. L. Powell
First Appearance October 27

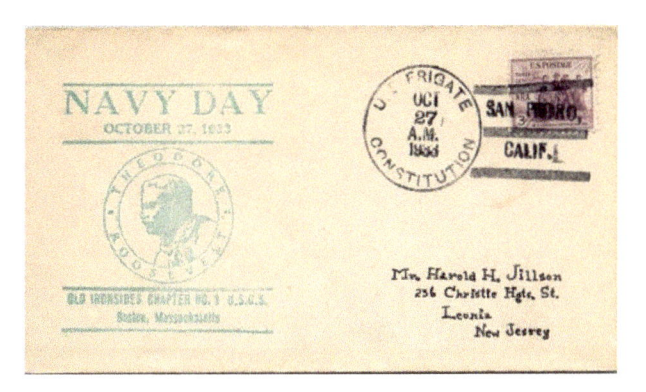

PRIVATE: Cachet sponsor John Paul Jones Chapter No. 2 USCS
First Appearance October 27

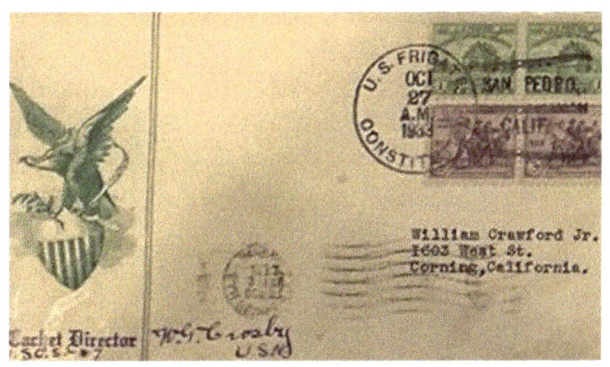

PRIVATE: Cachet sponsor W. G. Crosby
First Appearance October 27

OFFICIAL: Cachet sponsor Chamber of Commerce
First Appearance November 2 (2084 covers)

NOTE: In the early morning hours of Nov. 1, Harry Moore was involved in a auto accident in Los Angeles. Due to a severe gash to his arm, and possible other injuries, he was sent to the hospital ship USS Relief. In the meantime, F. A. Majerowski assumed his duties on the *Constitution* as Mail Clerk. Thus, the cancellations applied between Nov. 1 and approximately Nov. 14 when Moore returned, were applied by Majerowski.

AVALON, CALIFORNIA: November 2, 1933 – November 2, 1933
KILLER BARS: AVALON
              CALIF

OFFICIAL: Cachet sponsor Avalon Business Men's Association
First Appearance November 2 (2002 covers)

SAN DIEGO, CALIFORNIA: November 3, 1933 - March 30, 1934
Also at this port: S1, S2, S3, S4, S5, S6, S7, E9, E10a, E11, E12 - E23
KILLER BARS: SAN DIEGO
              CALIFORNIA

OFFICIAL: Cachet sponsor Chamber of Commerce
First Appearance November 3 (1292 covers)

OFFICIAL: Cachet sponsor Chamber of Commerce
First Appearance November 4 (3164 covers)

PRIVATE: Cachet sponsor Dr. H. H. Kretzler
First Appearance November 6 (50 cards)

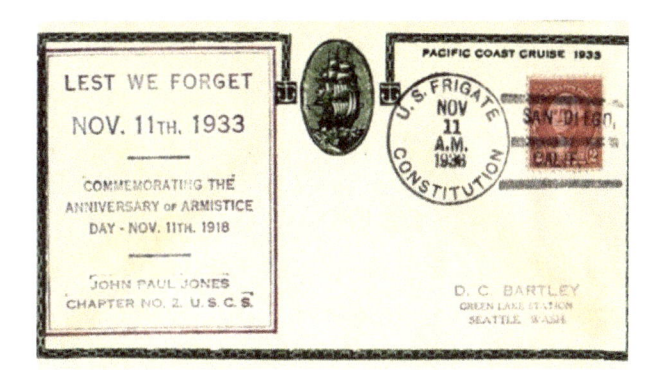

PRIVATE: Cachet sponsor John Paul Jones Chapter 2 USCS
First Appearance November 11

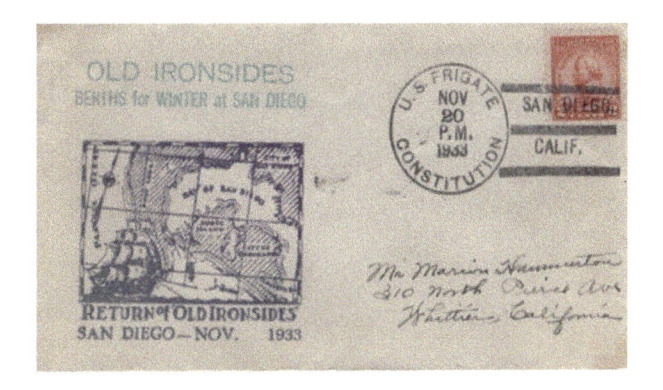

OFFICIAL: Cachet sponsor Chamber of Commerce
First Appearance November 20 (337 covers)

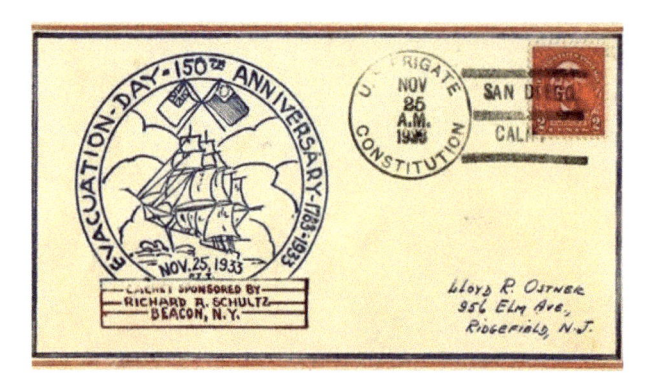

PRIVATE: Cachet sponsor Richard R. Schultz
First Appearance November 25

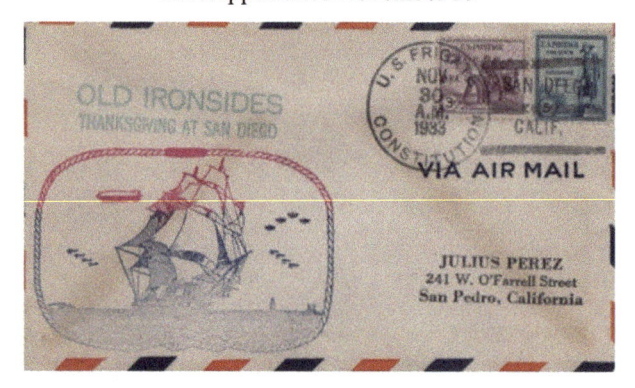

OFFICIAL: Cachet sponsor Chamber of Commerce
First Appearance November 30 (337 covers)

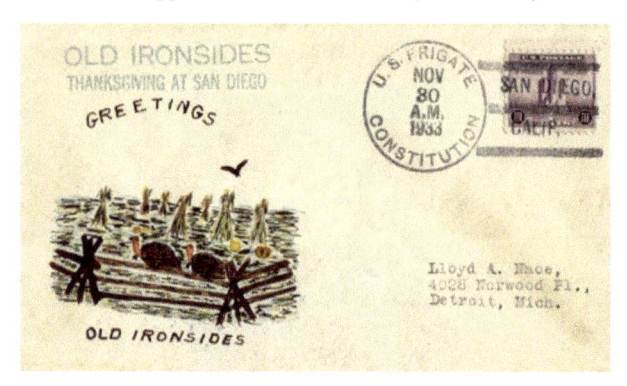

PRIVATE: Cachet sponsor unknown
First Appearance November 30

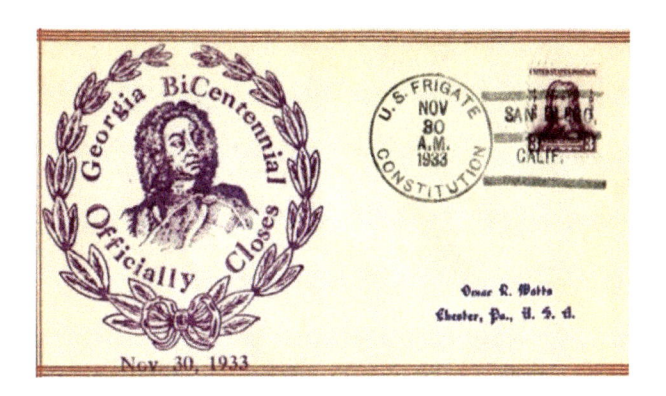

PRIVATE: Cachet sponsor unknown
First Appearance November 30

PRIVATE: Cachet sponsor Chapter 46 USCS
First Appearance November 30

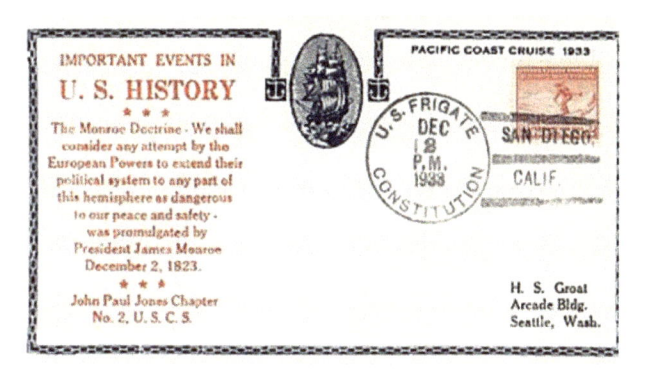

PRIVATE: Cachet sponsor John Paul Jones Chapter 2 USCS
First Appearance December 2

PRIVATE: Cachet sponsor Dr. H. H. Kretzler
First Appearance December 11 (100 cards)

OFFICIAL: Cachet sponsor unknown
First Appearance December 25 (2034 covers)

PRIVATE: Cachet sponsor Fighting Bob Evans Chapter #7, USCS
First Appearance December 25

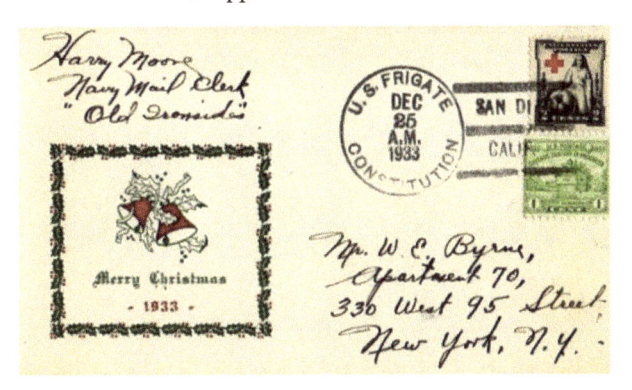

PRIVATE: Cachet sponsor unknown
First Appearance December 25

PRIVATE: Cachet sponsor unknown
First Appearance December 25

PRIVATE: Cachet sponsor unknown
First Appearance December 25

PRIVATE: Cachet sponsor unknown
First Appearance December 25

PRIVATE: Cachet sponsor unknown
First Appearance December 25

PRIVATE: Cachet sponsor Dr. H. H. Kretzler
First Appearance December 26 (100 cards)

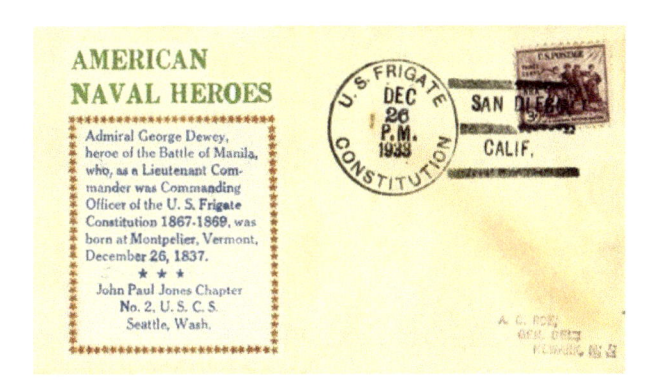

PRIVATE: Cachet sponsor John Paul Jones Chapter No. 2 USCS
First Appearance December 26 (80 covers)

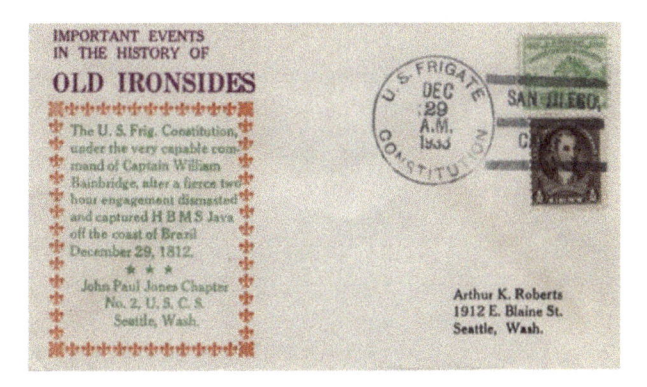

PRIVATE: Cachet sponsor John Paul Jones Chapter No. 2 USCS
First Appearance December 29 (77 covers)

PRIVATE: Cachet sponsor Frank I. Morse
First Appearance December 29 (75 covers)

PRIVATE: Cachet sponsor Frank I. Morse
First Appearance December 29

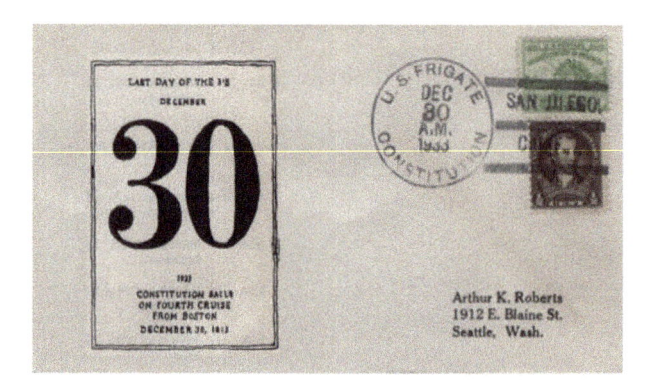

PRIVATE: Cachet sponsor Frank I. Morse
First Appearance December 30 (25 covers)

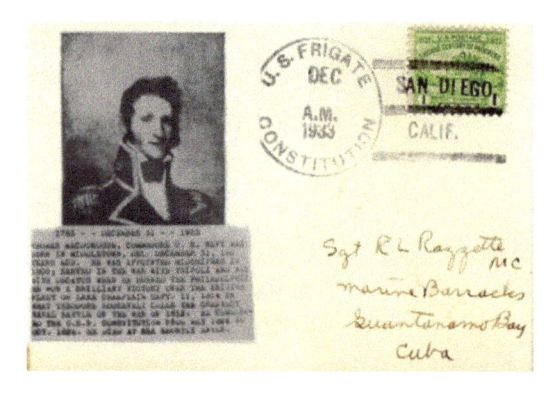

PRIVATE: Cachet sponsor Dr. H. H. Kretzler
First Appearance December 31 (100 cards)

1934

SAN DIEGO, CALIFORNIA: Nov 3, 1933 – March 20, 1934 (cont)
KILLER BARS: **SAN DIEGO**
CALIF

PRIVATE: Cachet sponsor unknown
First Appearance January 1

OFFICIAL: Cachet sponsor unknown
First Appearance January 1

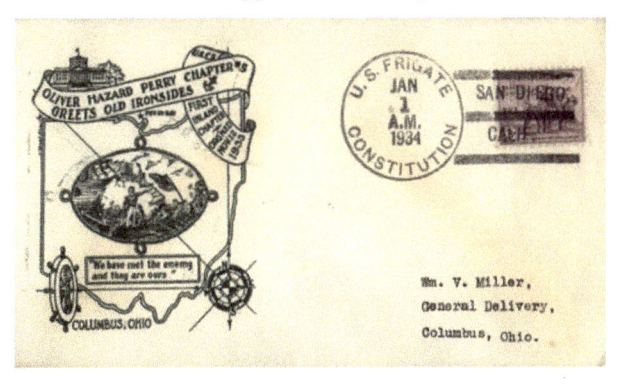

PRIVATE: Cachet sponsor Oliver Hazard Perry Chapter #5
First Appearance January 1

140

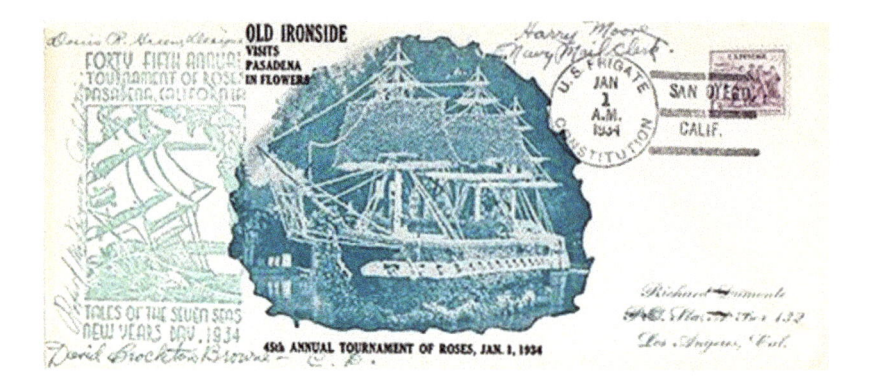

PRIVATE: Cachet sponsor David Brockton Browne
First Appearance January 1

PRIVATE: Cachet sponsor Dr. H. H. Kretzler
First Appearance January 5 (100 cards)

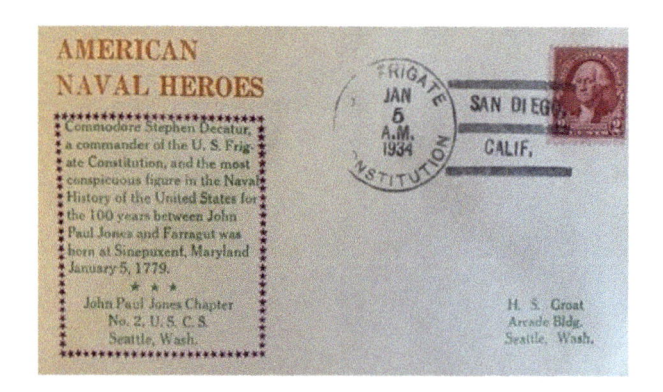

PRIVATE: Cachet sponsor John Paul Jones Chapter No. 2 USCS
First Appearance January 5 (54 covers)

142

PRIVATE: Cachet sponsor E. J. Wilson
First Appearance January 5

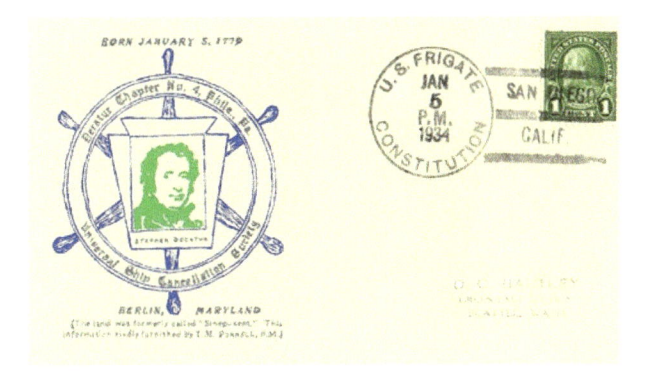

PRIVATE: Cachet sponsor Decatur Chapter No. 4 USCS
First Appearance January 5

PRIVATE: Cachet sponsor William V. Miller
First Appearance January 30

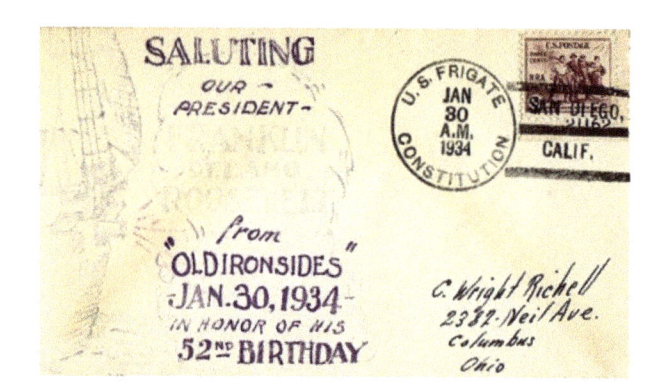

PRIVATE: Cachet sponsor Donald A. Schramm & C. Wright Richell
First Appearance January 30 (30 covers)

PRIVATE: Cachet sponsor Donald A. Schramm & C. Wright Richell
First Appearance Junuary 30 (20 covers)

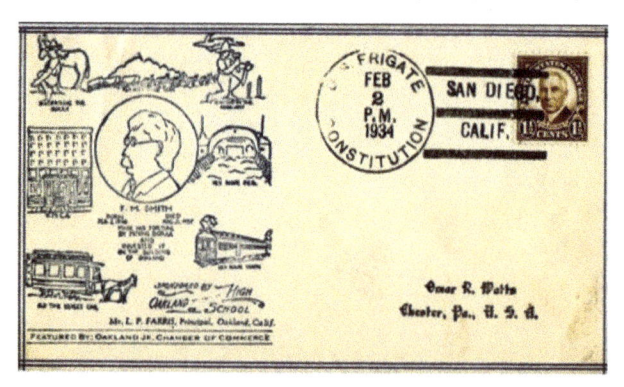

PRIVATE: Cachet sponsor Oakland Jr. Chamber Commerce
First Appearance February 2

OFFICIAL: Cachet sponsor H. Grimsland
First Appearance of Envelope Cachet E27 February 6

PRIVATE: Cachet sponsor E. J. Wilson
First Appearance February 9

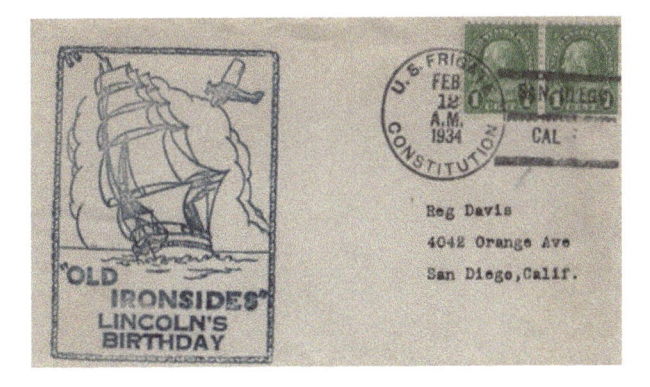

OFFICIAL: Cachet sponsor unknown
First Appearance February 12 (1710 covers)

PRIVATE: Cachet sponsor unknown
First Appearance February 12

PRIVATE: Cachet sponsor unknown
First Appearance February 12

PRIVATE: Cachet sponsor William V. Miller
First Appearance February 12

PRIVATE: Cachet sponsor Donald A. Schramm & C. Wright Richell
First Appearance February 14 (30 Covers)

PRIVATE: Cachet sponsor unknown
First Appearance February 14

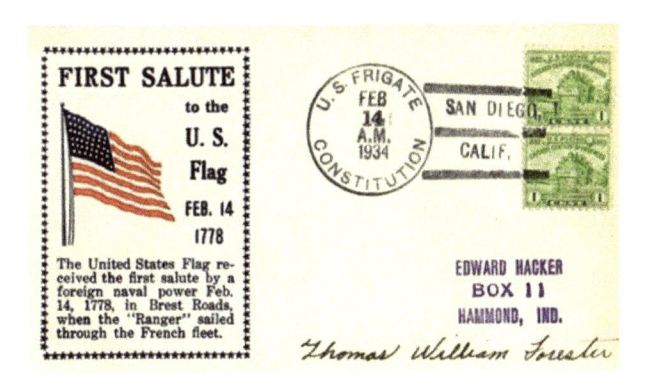

PRIVATE: Cachet sponsor Edward Hacker
First Appearance February 14

PRIVATE: Cachet sponsor unknown
First Appearance February 16

PRIVATE: Cachet sponsor John Paul Jones Chapter No. 2 USCS
First Appearance February 16 (40 covers)

Wooden Greeting Card made available to *Constitution* visitors in 1933

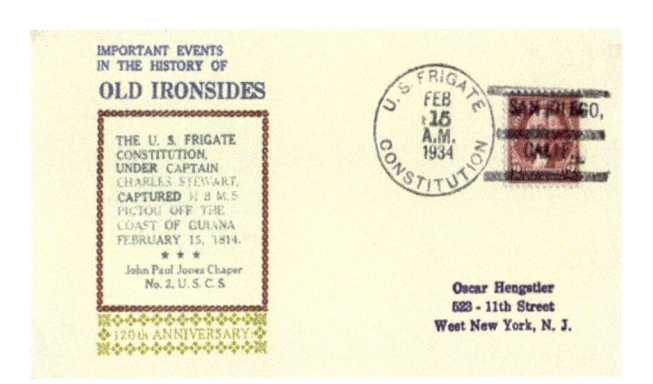

PRIVATE: Cachet sponsor John Paul Jones Chapter No. 2 USCS
First Appearance February 16 (32 covers)

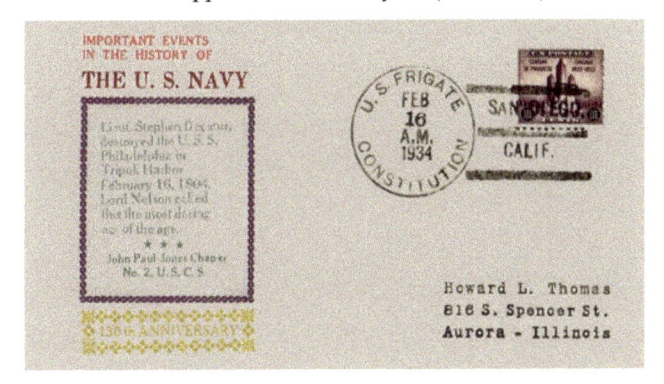

PRIVATE: Cachet sponsor John Paul Jones Chapter No. 2 USCS
First Appearance February 16 (40 covers)

PRIVATE: Cachet sponsor Donald A. Schramm & C. Wright Richell
First Appearance February 16 (40 covers)

PRIVATE: Cachet sponsor T. H. Holcombe, 4th
First Appearance February 16

PRIVATE: Cachet sponsor Donald A. Schramm & C. Wright Richell
First Appearance February 18 (35 covers)

PRIVATE: Cachet sponsor Donald A. Schramm & C. Wright Richell
First Appearance February 19 (35 covers)

PRIVATE: Cachet sponsor William V. Miller
First Appearance February 19

PRIVATE: Cachet sponsor Donald A. Schramm & C. Wright Richell
First Appearance February 19 (35 covers)

PRIVATE: Cachet sponsor Leonard Gilman
First Appearance February 19 (35 covers)

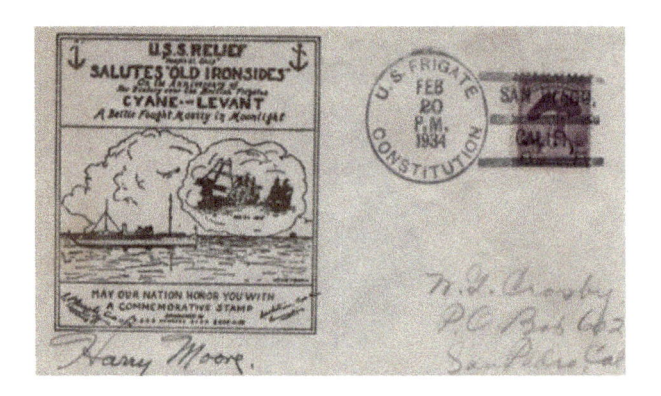

OFFICIAL: Cachet sponsor W. P. D'Amour, Aaron H. G. Voss & W. G. Crosby
First Appearance February 20 (551 covers)

PRIVATE: Cachet sponsor Donald A. Schramm & C. Wright Richell
First Appearance February 20 (35 covers)

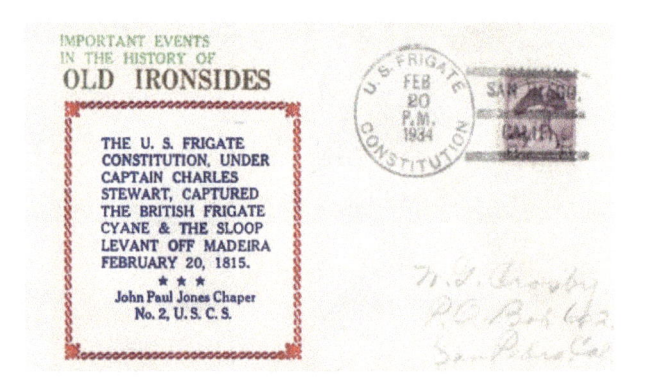

PRIVATE: Cachet sponsor John Paul Jones Chapter No. 2 USCS
First Appearance February 20 (30 covers)

PRIVATE: Cachet sponsor Leonard Gilman
First Appearance February 20 (200 covers)

PRIVATE: Cachet sponsor Edward Hacker
First Appearance February 20

PRIVATE: Cachet sponsor H. Grimsland
First Appearance February 20

OFFICIAL: Cachet sponsor unknown
(Overprint in style used by John Paul Jones Chapter No. 2 USCS)
First Appearance February 20

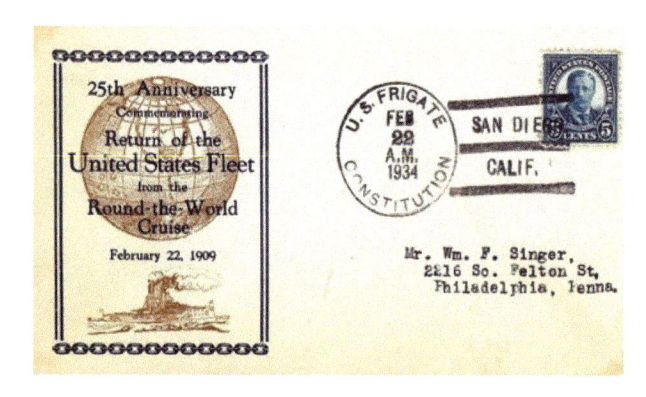

PRIVATE: Cachet sponsor unknown
First Appearance February 22

PRIVATE: Cachet sponsor Frank I. Morse
First Appearance February 22 (25 covers)

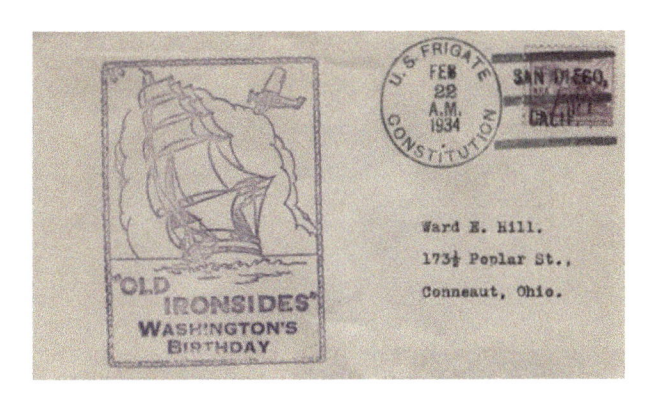

OFFICIAL: Cachet sponsor unknown
First Appearance February 22 (1850 covers)

PRIVATE: Cachet sponsor unknown
First Appearance February 22

PRIVATE: Cachet sponsor unknown
First Appearance February 22

PRIVATE: Cachet sponsor W. G. Crosby
First Appearance February 22

OFFICIAL: Cachet sponsor Veterans of Foreign Wars, District No.1
First Appearance February 25 (250 covers)

PRIVATE: Cachet sponsor E. J. Wilson
First Appearance February 26

PRIVATE: Cachet sponsor Donald A. Schramm & C. Wright Richell
First Appearance February 28 (40 covers)

PRIVATE: Cachet sponsor Donald A. Schramm & C. Wright Richell
First Appearance March 4

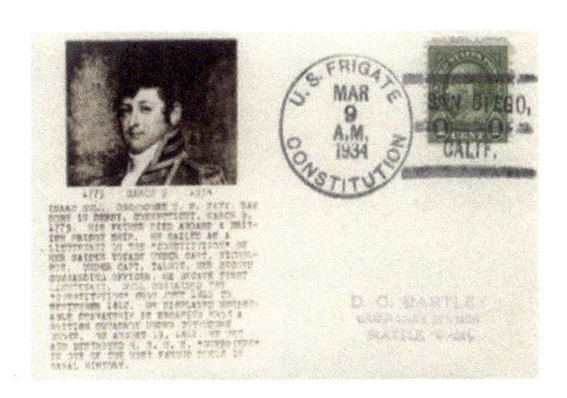

PRIVATE: Cachet sponsor Dr. H. H. Kretzler
First Appearance March 9 (100 cards)

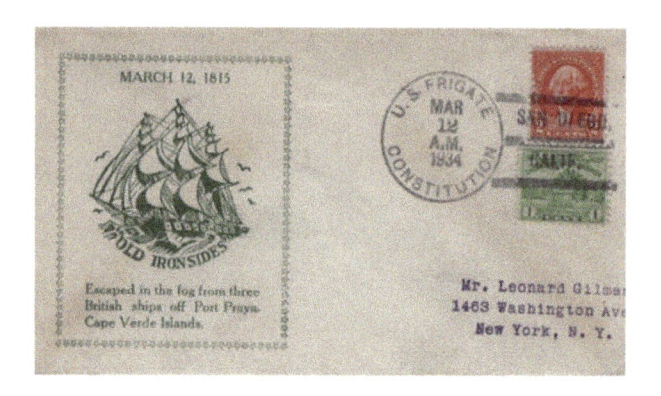

PRIVATE: Cachet sponsor Leonard Gilman
First Appearance March 12 (165 covers)

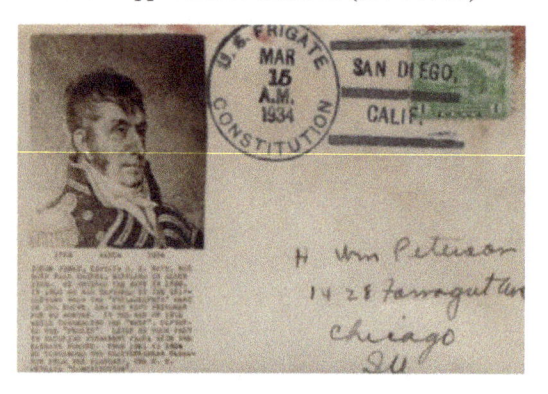

PRIVATE: Cachet sponsor Dr. H. H. Kretzler
First Appearance March 15 (100 cards)

OFFICIAL: Cachet sponsor John Gill
First Appearance Envelope Cachet E7b March 17

OFFICIAL: Cachet sponsor John Gill
First Appearance Envelope Cachet E10d March 17

PRIVATE: Cachet sponsor Fighting Bob Evans Chapter No. 7 USCS
First Appearance March 17

PRIVATE: Cachet sponsor Donald A. Schramm & C. Wright Richell
First Appearance March 17

OFFICIAL: Cachet sponsor John Paul Jones Chapter No. 2 USCS
First Appearance March 20 (820 covers)

OFFICIAL: Cachet sponsor Fighting Bob Evans Chapter No. 7 USCS
First Appearance March 20
NOTE: Most of these cachet covers were canceled with the San Pedro, California postmark.

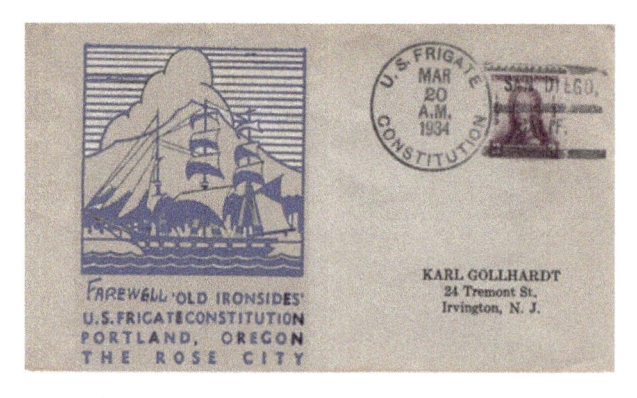

OFFICIAL: Cachet sponsor Myron F. McCamley
First Appearance March 20

OFFICIAL: Cachet sponsor Edward E. Bryan
First Appearance March 20

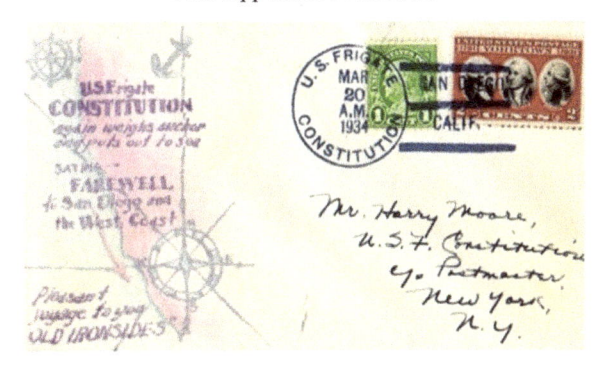

PRIVATE: Cachet sponsor Donald A. Schramm & C. Wright Richell
First Appearance March 20 (35 covers)

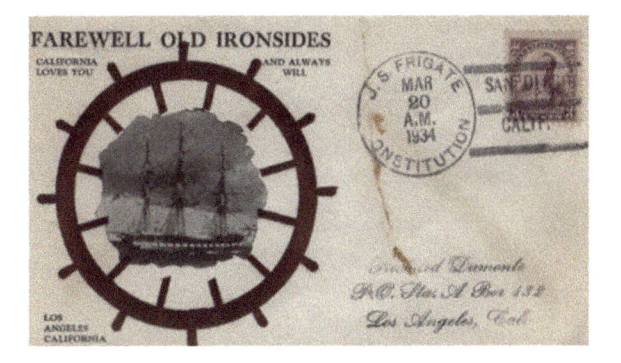

PRIVATE: Cachet sponsor Richard P. Dumonte
First Appearance March 20

PRIVATE: Cachet sponsor Alex Hesse Jr & William J. Hager
First Appearance March 20

PRIVATE: Cachet sponsor Frank I Morse
First Appearance March 20

OFFICIAL: Cachet sponsor Chamber of Commerce
First Appearance March 20 (4870 Covers)

PRIVATE: Cachet sponsor Frank I Morse
First Appearance March 20

PRIVATE: Cachet sponsor Frank I Morse
First Appearance March 20

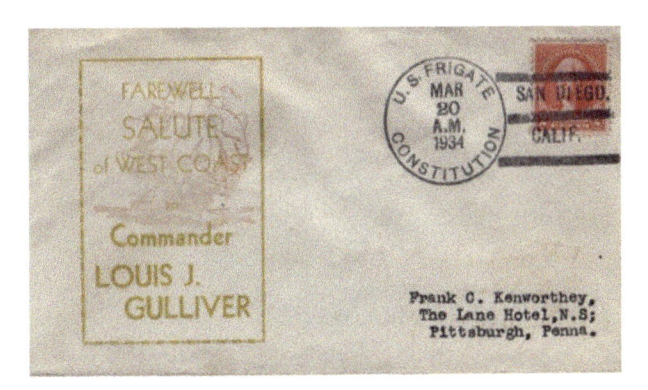

PRIVATE: Cachet sponsor Frank I Morse
First Appearance March 20

SAN DIEGO HARBOR: March 20, 1934
KILLER BARS: SAN DIEGO
　　　　　　　　HARBOR

PRIVATE: Cachet Sponsor Frank I. Morse
First Appearance March 20

PRIVATE: Cachet sponsor Harry Moore
First Appearance March 20

Constitution on way to Panama Canal

ENROUTE TO BALBOA, CANAL ZONE
Also at this port: S1, S6, E27
KILLER BARS: EN ROUTE
BALBOA, C.Z.

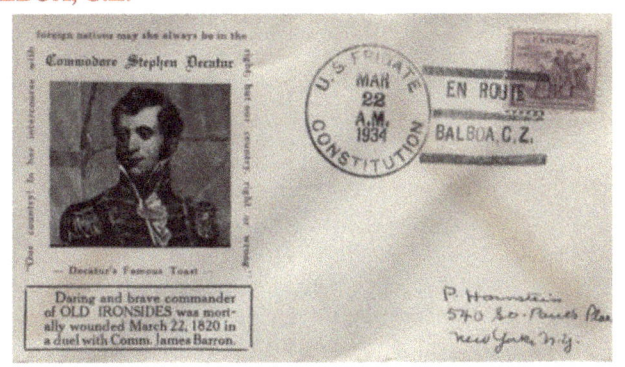

PRIVATE: Cachet sponsor Leonard Gilman
First Appearance March 22

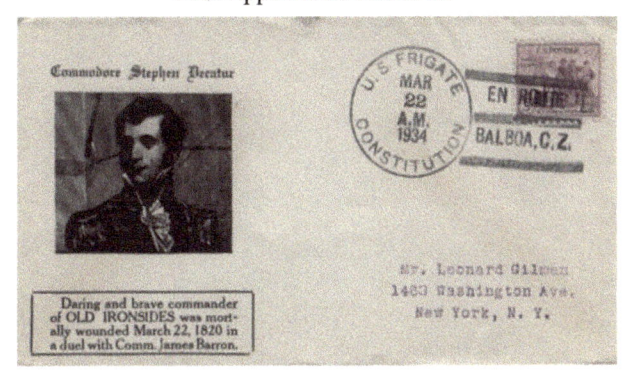

PRIVATE: Cachet sponsor Leonard Gilman
First Appearance March 22

Souvenir pinback *Constitution* Centennial Anniversary
Boston, MA - October 1897

ENROUTE TO BALBOA, CANAL ZONE
Also at this port: S4, E11, E27
KILLER BARS: LAT. 16-26 N.
LONG. 99-45 W

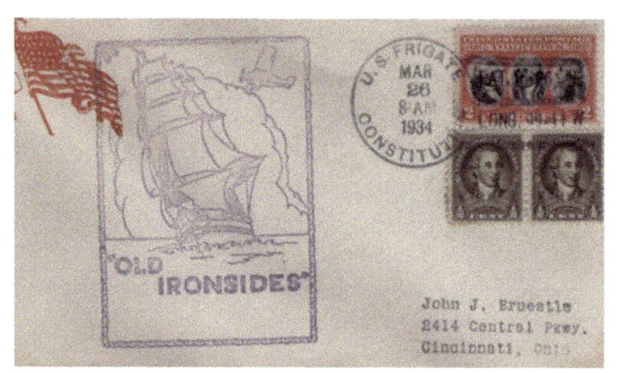

First Appearance March 26

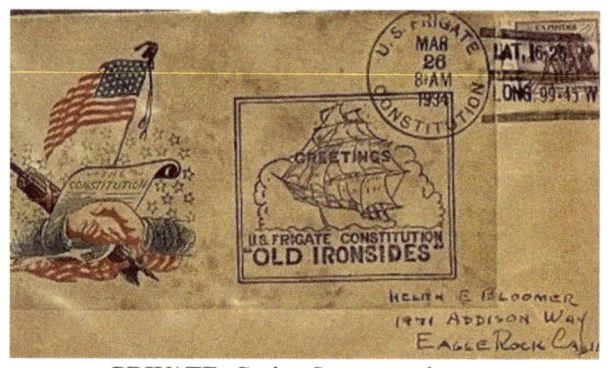

PRIVATE: Cachet Sponsor unknown
First Appearance March 26

ENROUTE TO BALBOA, CANAL ZONE
Also at this port: S3, S5, S6, E10a, E11, E27
KILLER BARS: AT SEA

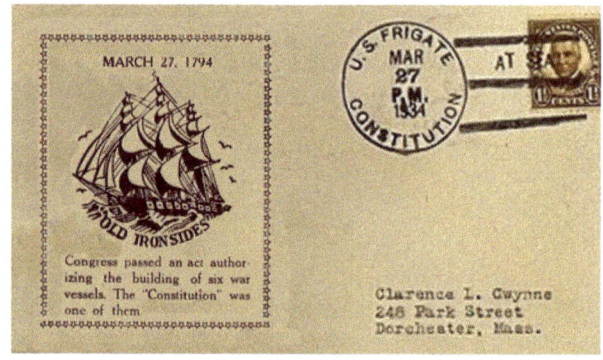

PRIVATE: Cachet sponsor Leonard Gilman
First Appearance March 27 (68 covers)

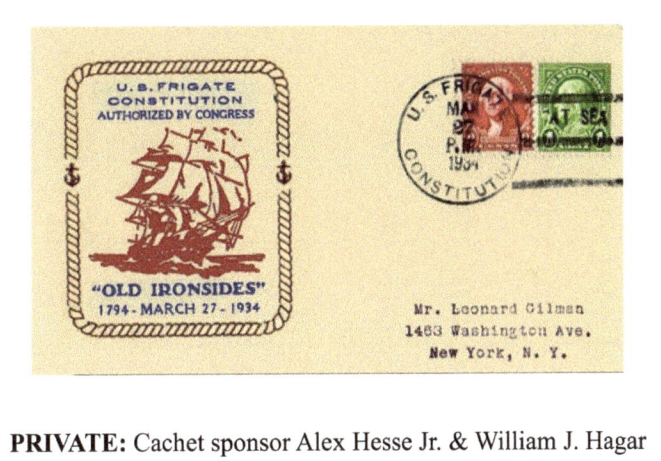

PRIVATE: Cachet sponsor Alex Hesse Jr. & William J. Hagar
First Appearance March 27

PRIVATE: Cachet sponsor Frank I. Morse
First Appearance March 27

PRIVATE: Cachet sponsor Julius W. Hulff
First Appearance March 27

ENROUTE TO BALBOA, CANAL ZONE
Also at this port: S4, S6
**KILLER BARS: GULF OF
              TEHUANTEPEC**

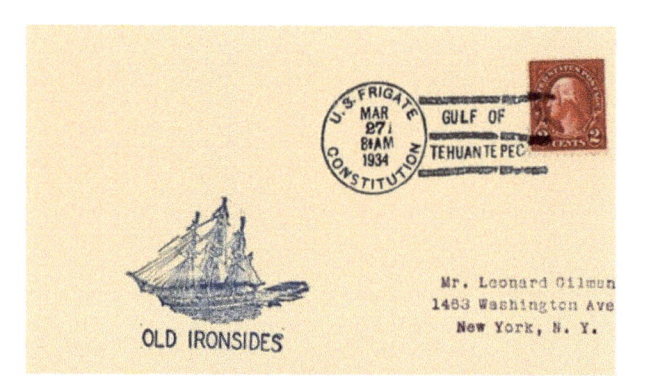

First Appearance March 27

ENROUTE TO BALBOA, CANAL ZONE
Also at this port: S3, S6, E27
**KILLER BARS: OFF COAST OF
              REP. PANAMA**

PRIVATE: Cachet sponsor Sarah Litton
First Appearance April 1

BALBOA, CANAL ZONE; April 2, 1934 – April 7, 1934
Also at this port: S1, S2, S3, S4, S5, S6, S7, E10a, E11, E27
KILLER BARS: BALBOA
               CANAL ZONE

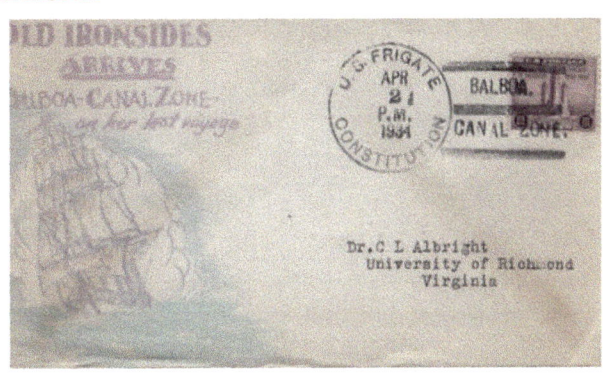

PRIVATE: Cachet sponsor Donald A. Schramm & C. Wright Richell
First Appearance April 2 (35 covers)

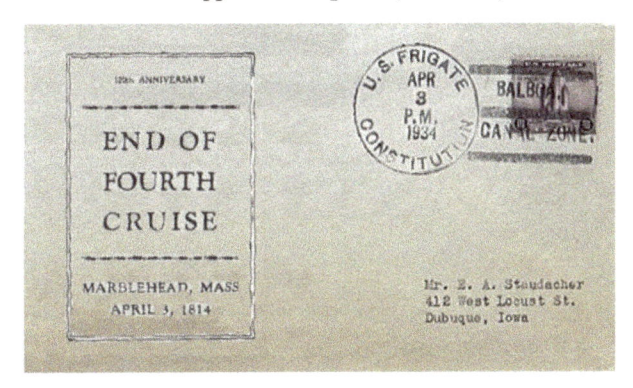

PRIVATE: Cachet sponsor Frank I. Morse
First Appearance April 3 (50 covers)

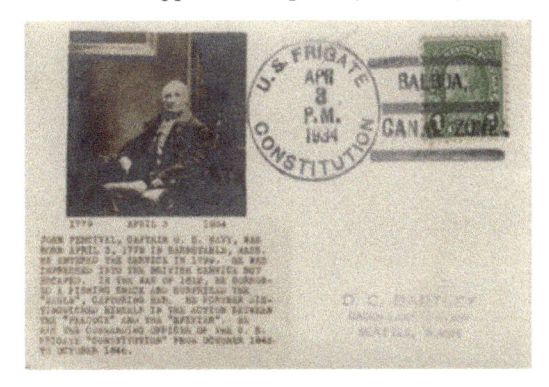

PRIVATE: Cachet sponsor Dr, H. H. Kretzler
First Appearance April 3 (100 cards)

OFFICIAL: Cachet sponsor Donald A. Schramm & C. Wright Richell
First Appearance Envelope Cachet E28 April 4

PRIVATE: Cachet sponsor Donald A. Schramm & C. Wright Richell
First Appearance April 4 (35 covers)

PRIVATE: Cachet sponsor Donald A. Schramm & C. Wright Richell
First Appearance April 4 (35 covers)

PASSAGE THROUGH PANAMA CANAL; April 7, 1934
Also at this port: S6, E11
KILLER BARS: TRANSIT PED
                MIGUEL LOCKS

OFFICIAL: Cachet sponsor Boy Scouts of the Canal Zone
First Appearance April 7 (A.M.)

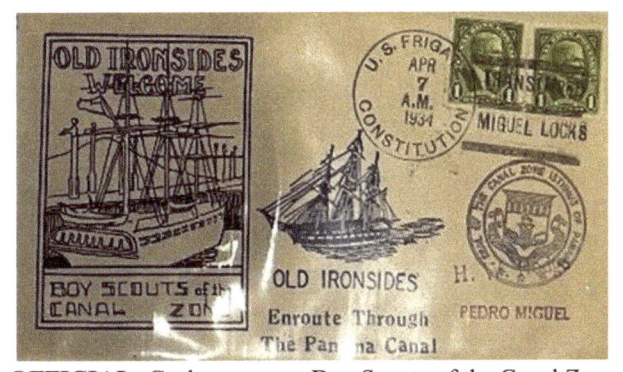

OFFICIAL: Cachet sponsor Boy Scouts of the Canal Zone
First Appearance April 7 (A.M.)

Constitution passing through Panama Canal locks

PASSAGE THROUGH PANAMA CANAL: April 7, 1934
Also at this port: S1, S4, S5
KILLER BARS: TRANSIT OF
　　　　　　　　PANAMA CANAL

OFFICIAL: Cachet sponsor Harry Moore
First Appearance April 7

CRISTOBAL, CANAL ZONE; April 7, 1934 – April 8, 1934
Also at this port: S1, S2, S3, S4, S5, S6, S7, E9, E10a, E11, E27
KILLER BARS: CRISTOBAL.
　　　　　　　　CANAL ZONE

PRIVATE: Cachet sponsor Frank I. Morse
First Appearance April 7 (30 covers)

PRIVATE: Cachet sponsor William V. Miller
First Appearance April 7

First Appearance April 7

ENROUTE TO ST. PETERSBURG, FLORIDA
Also at this port: S1, S3, S7, E27
KILLER BARS: LAT. 15-36
                LONG. 81-06

First Appearance April 10

ST. PETERSBURG, FLORIDA; April 14, 1934 – April 23, 1934
Also at this port: S1, S2, S3, S4, S5, S6, S7, E9, E10a, E11, E27
KILLER BARS: ST. PETERS-
                BURG, FLA

PRIVATE: Cachet sponsor Frank I. Morse
First Appearance April 14

172

PRIVATE: Cachet sponsor Donald A. Schramm & C. Wright Richell
First Appearance April 14 (35 covers)

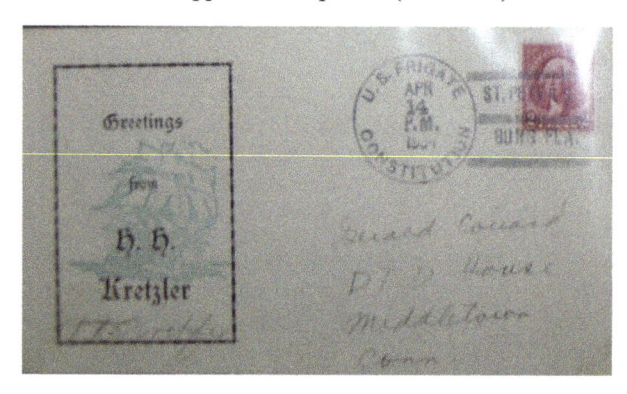

OFFICIAL: Cachet sponsor Dr. H. H. Kretzler
First Appearance April 14

OFFICIAL: Cachet sponsor Press of Historical Aeronautical Assn
First Appearance April 14

OFFICIAL: Cachet sponsor William V. Miller
First Appearance April 14

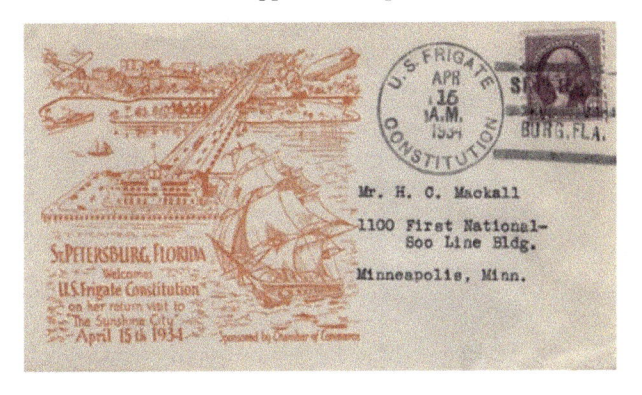

OFFICIAL: Cachet sponsor Chamber of Commerce
First Appearance April 15 (5,078 covers)

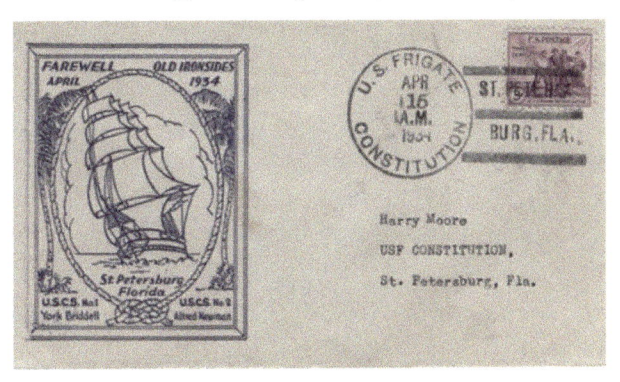

OFFICIAL: Cachet sponsor York Briddell & Alfred E. Newman
First Appearance April 15 (625 covers)

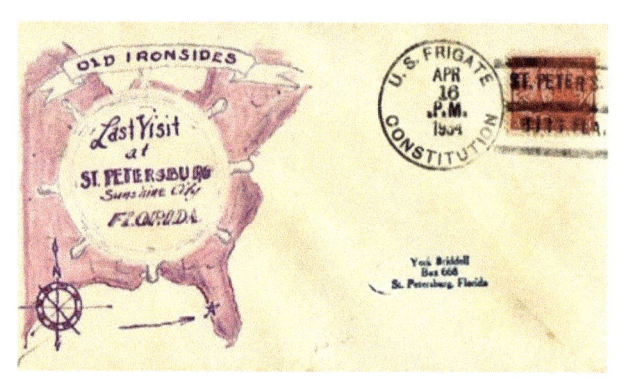

PRIVATE: Cachet sponsor Donald A. Schramm & C. Wright Richell
First Appearance April 15

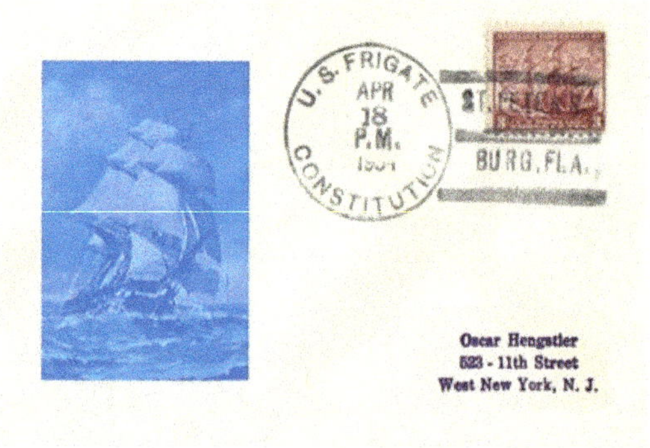

PRIVATE: Cachet sponsor Frank I. Morse
First Appearance April 18

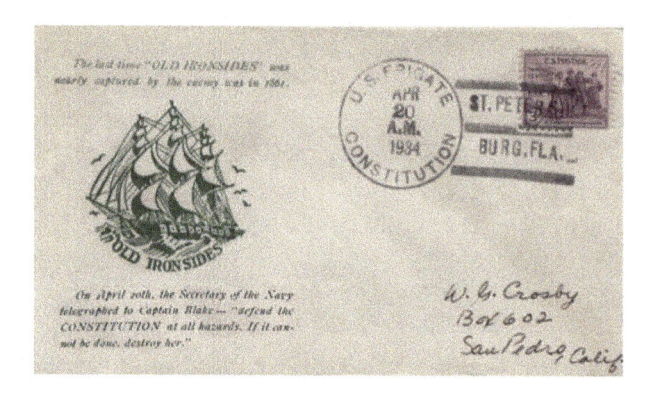

PRIVATE: Cachet sponsor Leonard Gilman
First Appearance April 20 (70 covers)

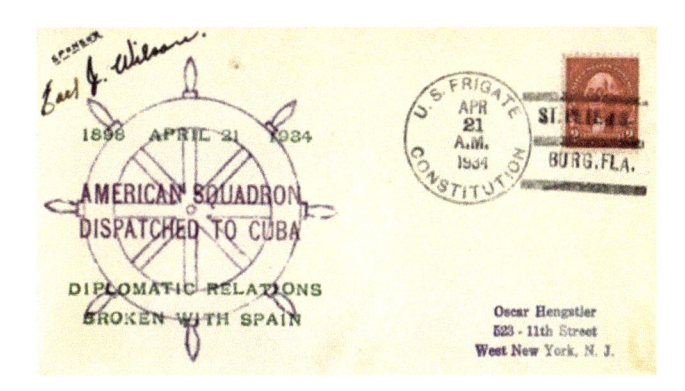

PRIVATE: Cachet sponsor Earl J. Wilson
First Appearance April 21

PRIVATE: Cachet sponsor Leonard Gilman
First Appearance April 21 (70 covers)

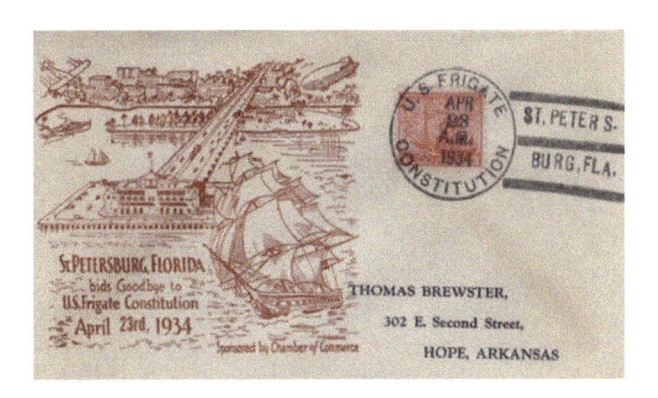

OFFICIAL: Cachet sponsor Chamber of Commerce
First Appearance April 23 (5583 covers)

PRIVATE: Cachet sponsor Alex Hesse Jr. & William J. Hagar
First Appearance April 23

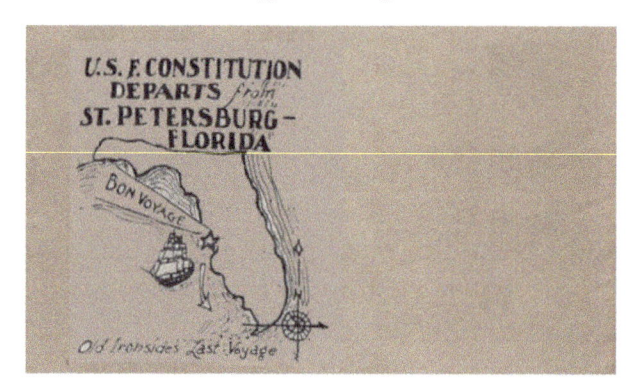

PRIVATE: Cachet sponsor Donald A. Schramm & C. Wright Richell
First Appearance April 23

PRIVATE: Cachet sponsor E. J. Wilson
First Appearance April 23

Charleston, South Carolina; April 27, 1934 – May 3, 1934
Also at this port: S1, S2, S3, S4, S5, S6, S7, E9, E10a, E11, E27
KILLER BARS: CHARLESTON
S.C.

OFFICIAL: Cachet sponsor Stamp Club of Charleston
First Appearance April 27 (2805 covers)

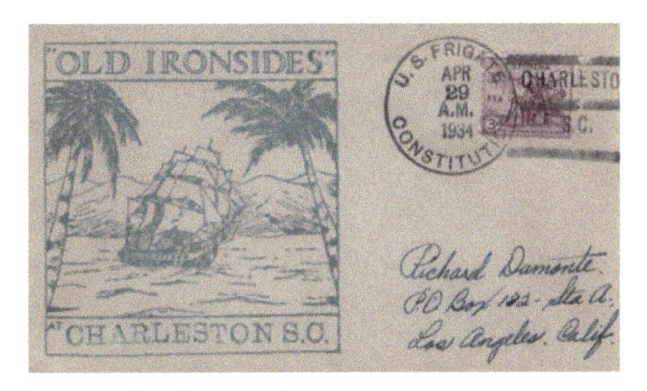

OFFICIAL: Cachet sponsor R. L. Razzette
First Appearance April 27

PRIVATE: Cachet sponsor Frank I. Morse
First Appearance April 27 (30 covers)

PRIVATE: Cachet sponsor Frank I. Morse
First Appearance April 27

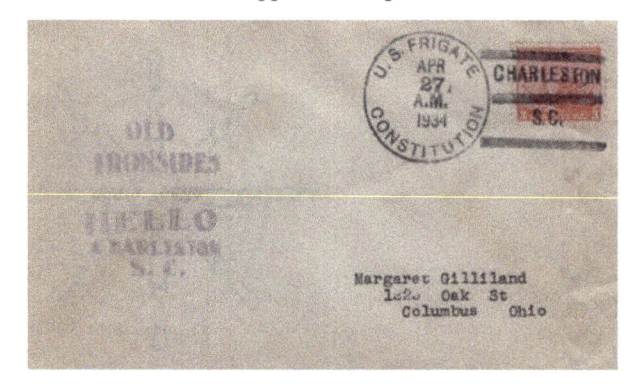

PRIVATE: Cachet sponsor Donald A. Schramm & C. Wright Richell
First Appearance April 27 (35 covers)

PRIVATE: Cachet sponsor E. E. Ward, Jr.
First Appearance April 27

PRIVATE: Cachet sponsor Alex Hesse Jr. & William J. Hagar
First Appearance April 27 (125 covers)

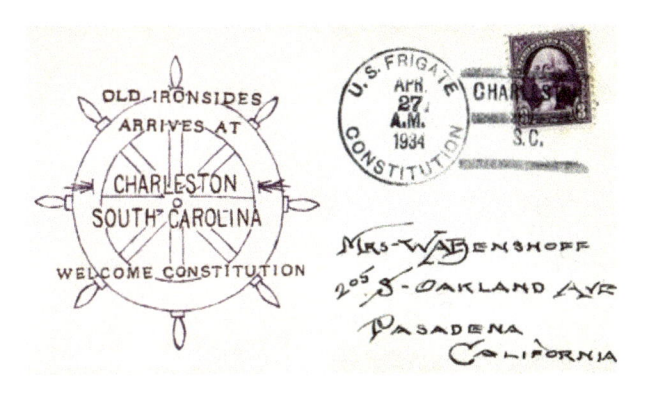

PRIVATE: Cachet sponsor E. J. Wilson
First Appearance April 27

PRIVATE: Cachet sponsor John Von Losberg
First Appearance April 30

PRIVATE: Cachet sponsor John Von Losberg
First Appearance April 30

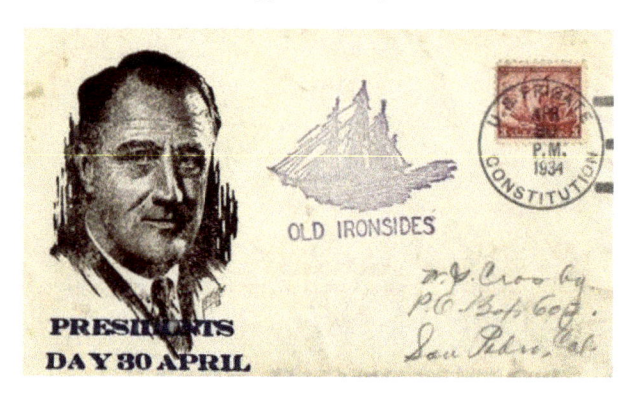

PRIVATE: Cachet sponsor W. G. Crosby
First Appearance April 30

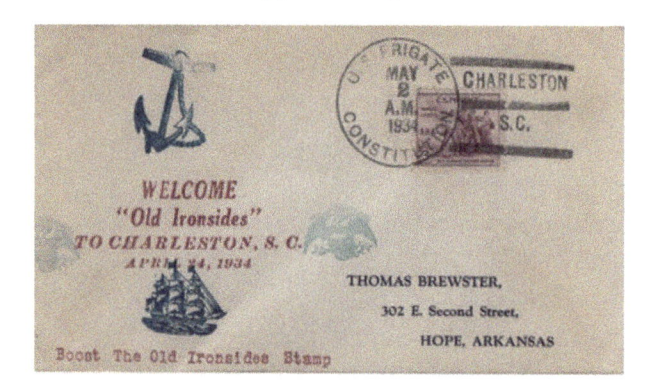

PRIVATE: Cachet sponsor E E. Ward, Jr.
First Appearance May 2

PRIVATE: Cachet sponsor E. J. Wilson
First Appearance May 3

Constitution approaching Boston Harbor

ENROUTE TO BOSTON, MASSACHUSETTS
Also at this port: S1, S2, S3, S4, S5, S6, S7, E9, E10a, E11, E27
KILLER BARS: **OFF CAPE HATTERAS**

NOTE: Most of the covers have "Homeward Bound H.M." written in cachet by the mail clerk, Harry Moore.

PRIVATE: Cachet sponsor Harry Moore
First Appearance May 4

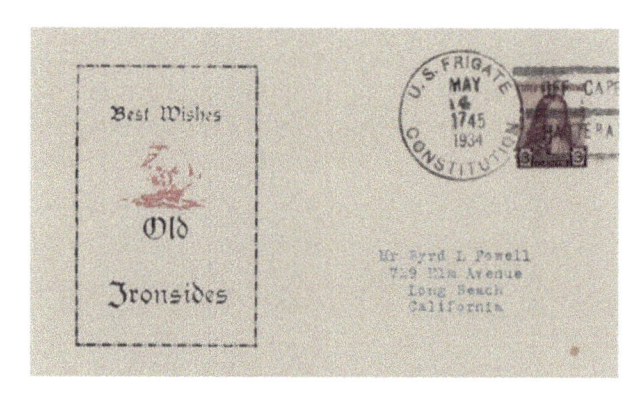

PRIVATE: Cachet sponsor Frank I. Morse
First Appearance May 4 (1745 covers)

PRIVATE: Cachet sponsor William V. Miller
First Appearance May 4

BOSTON, MASSACHUSETTS: May 7, 1934 – June 8, 1934
Also at this port: All 'Ship Cachets' and "Envelope Cachets'
KILLER BARS: BOSTON
                       MASS

OFFICIAL: Cachet sponsor Boston Newspaperman's Post #305 American Legion
First Appearance May 7 (1024 covers)

OFFICIAL: Cachet sponsor "Old Ironsides" Chapter No. 1 USCS
First Appearance May 7 (1253 covers)

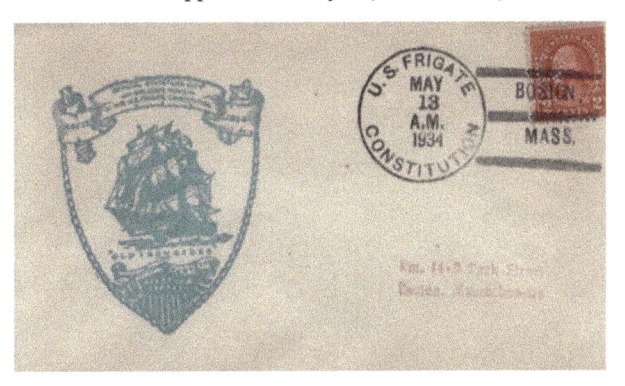

OFFICIAL: Cachet sponsor Boston Cachet Cover Committee
First Appearance May 7

184

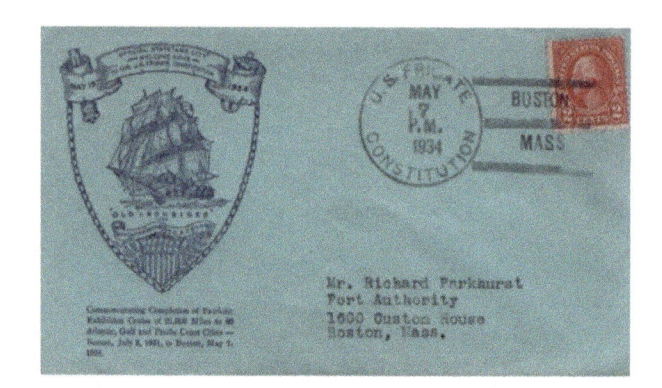

OFFICIAL: Cachet sponsor Boston Cachet Cover Committee
First Appearance May 7

PRIVATE: Cachet sponsor Frank I. Morse
First Appearance May 7

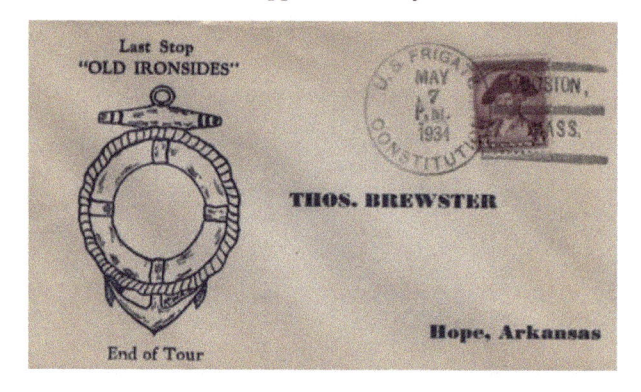

PRIVATE: Cachet sponsor John Dunlap
First Appearance May 7

PRIVATE: Cachet sponsor Donald A. Schramm & C. Wright Richell
First Appearance May 7 (35 covers)

PRIVATE: Cachet sponsor unknown
First Appearance May 7

PRIVATE: Cachet sponsor Oscar Hengstler
First Appearance May 7

PRIVATE: Cachet sponsor Oscar Hengstler
First Appearance May 7

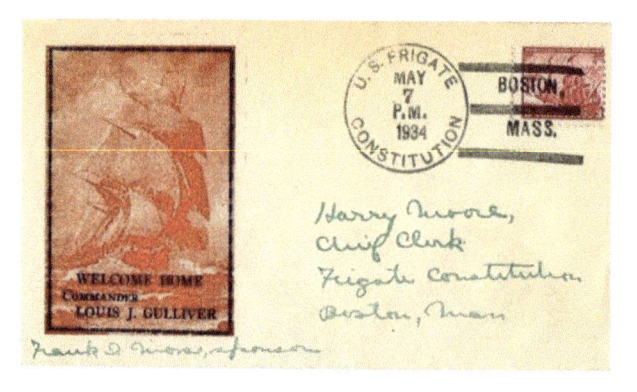

PRIVATE: Cachet sponsor Frank I. Morse
First Appearance May 7 (50 covers)

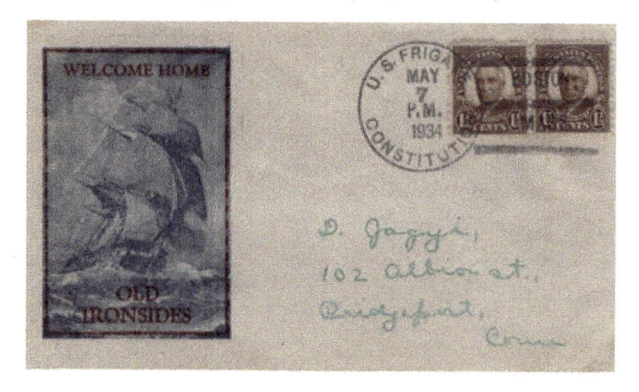

PRIVATE: Cachet sponsor Frank I. Morse
First Appearance May 7 (50 covers)

PRIVATE: Cachet sponsor Frank I. Morse
First Appearance May 7 (50 covers)

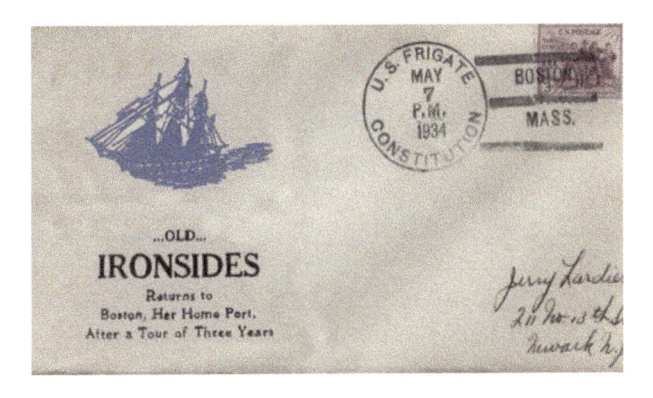

PRIVATE: Cachet sponsor Julius W. Hulff
First Appearance May 7 (25 covers)

PRIVATE: Cachet sponsor Oscar Hengstler
First Appearance May 7

PRIVATE: Cachet sponsor Dr. H. H. Kretzler
First Appearance May 7 (100 cards)

PRIVATE: Cachet sponsor unknown
First Appearance May 7

PRIVATE: Cachet sponsor Richard F. Hoffner
First Appearance May 7

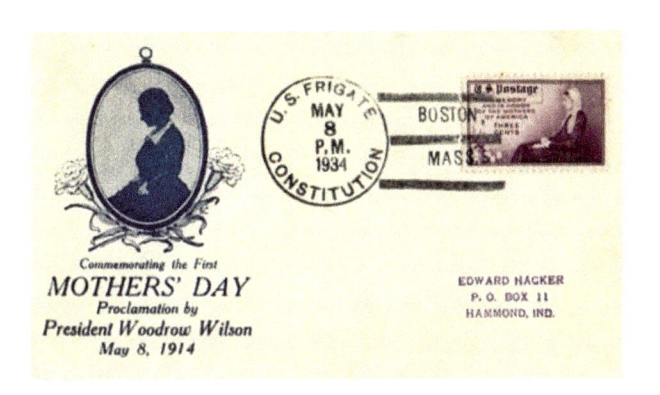

PRIVATE: Cachet sponsor unknown
First Appearance May 8

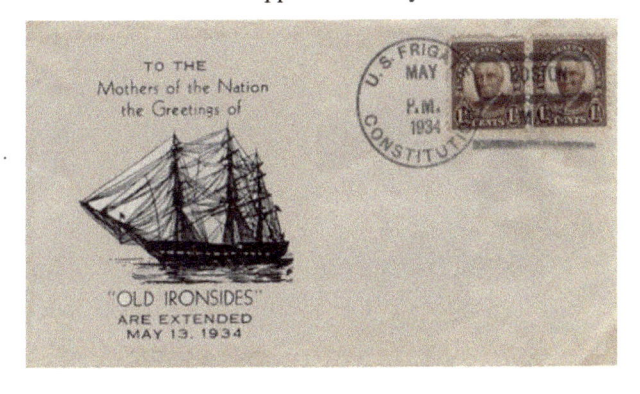

PRIVATE: Cachet sponsor John E. Gill
First Appearance May 13

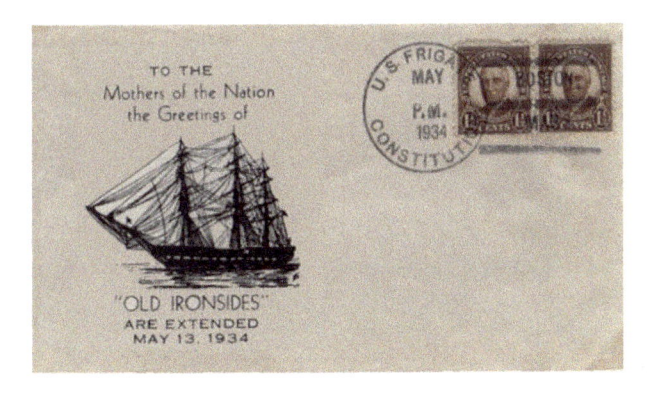

PRIVATE: Cachet Sponsor John E. Gill
(Previous cachet with overprinted "Mother's Day Poem)

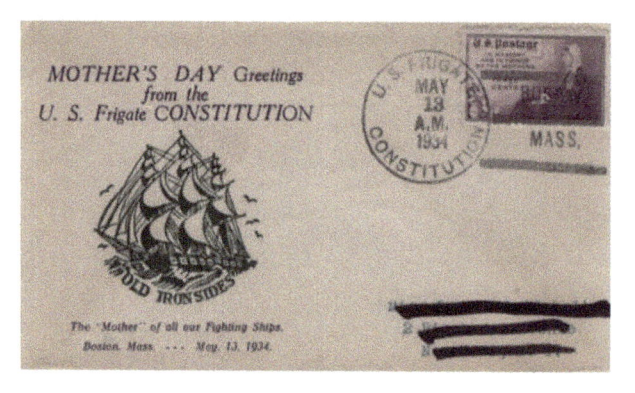

PRIVATE: Cachet sponsor Leonard Gilman
First Appearance May 13 (75 covers)

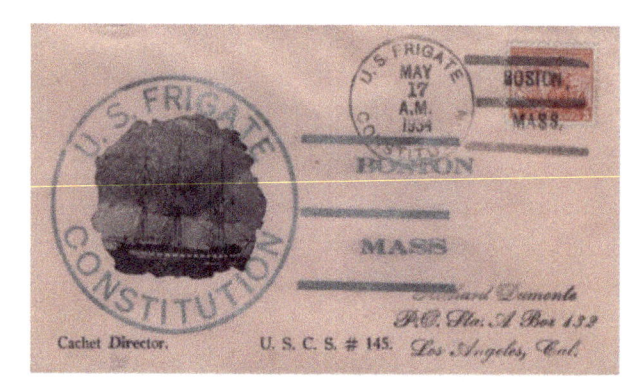

PRIVATE: Cachet sponsor Richard P. Dumonte
First Appearance May 13

PRIVATE: Cachet sponsor unknown
First Appearance May 13

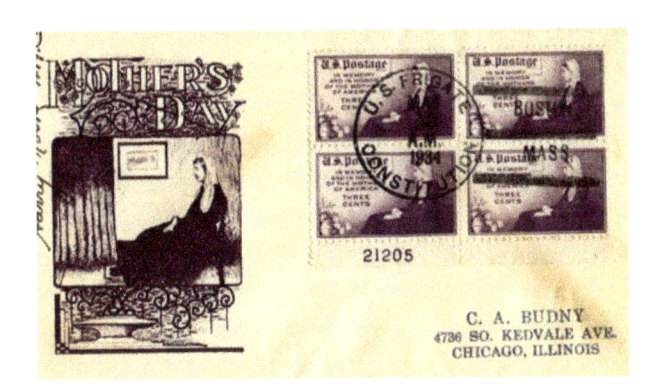

PRIVATE: Cachet sponsor unknown
First Appearance May 13

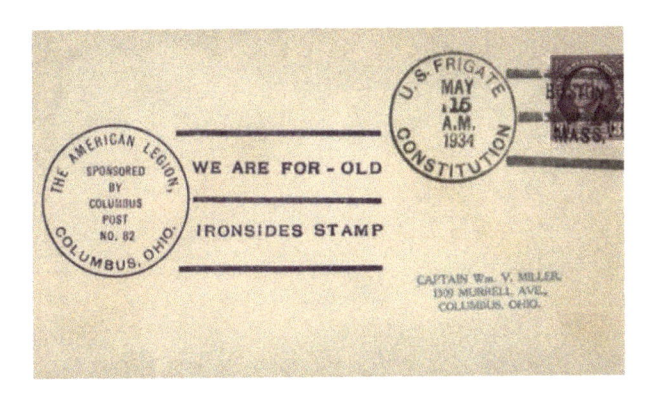

PRIVATE: Cachet sponsor William V. Miller
First Appearance May 15

PRIVATE: Cachet sponsor Roger A. Wentworth
First Appearance May 16

General Public Reception

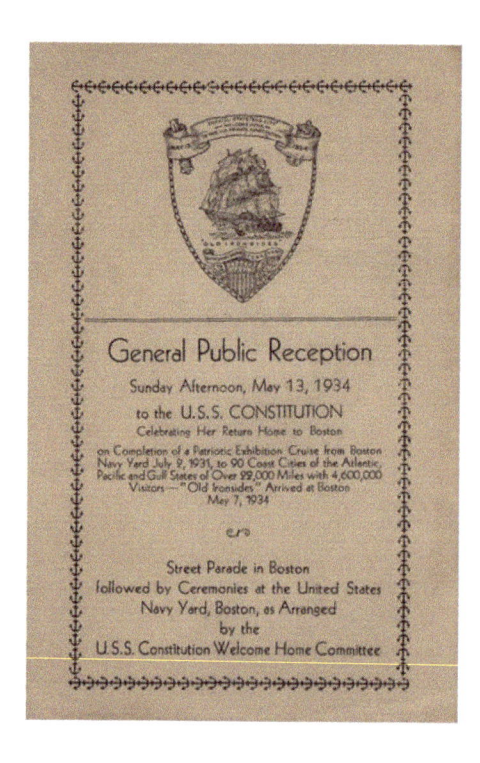

Sunday Afternoon, May 13, 1934
to the U.S.S. CONSTITUTION
Celebrating Her Return Home to Boston
on Completion of a Patriotic Exhibition Cruise from Boston Navy Yard July 2, 1931, to 90 Coast Cities of the Atlantic, Pacific and Gulf States of Over 22,000 Miles with 4,600,000 Visitors — "Old Ironsides" Arrived at Boston May 7, 1934

Street Parade in Boston
followed by Ceremonies at the United States
Navy Yard, Boston, as Arranged
by the
U.S.S. Constitution Welcome Home Committee

General Public Reception Program - May 13, 1934

Program For Navy Yard Exercises

Arranged and Conducted by the Citizens Committee by the Courtesy of the Commandant

ARRIVAL OF PARADE and Formation for Exercises.
PRELUDE—Selection by Band—"Stars and Stripes Forever."
WELCOME by Rear Admiral Henry H. Hough, U. S. Navy, Commandant of First Naval District.
INVOCATION by Rev. Robert P. Barry, Director of Catholic Charitable Bureau.
OPENING REMARKS by the Committee Chairman, Hon. John F. Fitzgerald.
SINGING by Municipal Choral Society.
 "Prayer of Thanksgiving" .... Kremser
 "To Thee O Country" .... Julius Eichberg
READING of "Old Ironsides" (Oliver Wendell Holmes), by Carmen Cefalo, 6th Grade, Eliot School, Boston.
PRESENTATION of Commander Louis J. Gulliver, U. S. Navy, Commanding U. S. S. Constitution; and the officers and crew.
MUSIC by the Band—"Anchors Aweigh".
READING of original poem—"Old Ironsides Returns", by Henry Gillen.
SOLO—"The American Hymn", by Lawrence Thornton.
PRESENTATION of Hon. Charles Francis Adams of Boston, Secretary of the Navy when the "Constitution" was recommissioned in 1931; Lieut. John A. Lord, U. S. N., Retired, of Bath, Me., supervisor of reconstruction of the ship; Technicians and workmen of the Navy Yard force, some of whom helped recondition the ship in 1931 and earlier.
THE COMMONWEALTH OF MASSACHUSETTS—Hon. Joseph B. Ely, Governor.
SOLO—"Columbia, Gem of the Ocean", Madame Rose Zulalian.
THE CITY OF BOSTON—Hon. Frederick W. Mansfield, Mayor.
CHORUS—"Hymn to America",
 "Unfold Ye Portals Everlasting".
PRESENTATION of Mayors and Chairmen of Selectmen.
ADDRESS—Capt. Thomas G. Frothingham.
SOLO—"Hail Columbia", Lawrence Thornton.
FINALE—"America"—Massed Bands—Chorus—Audience.
 "Colors".
 Assembly of Flags.
 Benediction—By Rev. Ernest J. Dennen, Archdeacon of Boston.
 "Star Spangled Banner".

PROGRAM (continued)

RADIO broadcast of the program—Station WNAC.
BAND—Roxbury Memorial High School.
MUNICIPAL CHORAL SOCIETY of the City of Boston, under direction of Lawrence E. O'Connor—"Hymn to America", words by Clara Endicott Sears; music by Mrs. M. H. Gulesian.
SOLOISTS—Madame Rose Zulalian, and Lawrence Thornton, accompanied by Edith Thornton.
READER of "Old Ironsides" specially selected from Eliot School, North End, Boston, celebrating its 100th anniversary this year.
USHERS—Officers of Boston High School Cadets.
AUDIENCE includes representatives of several of the cities and towns of the metropolitan Boston district, all of whom were invited to participate.
PIANO by courtesy of A. M. Hume Piano Company.
SPEAKERS' STAND by courtesy of City of Chelsea.

Parade in Boston

1:45 o'clock P.M., Sunday, May 13, 1934—Parade starts from Constitution Wharf, Commercial Street, and proceeds to Boston Navy Yard:

ROUTE—Constitution Wharf—to Atlantic Avenue—to State Street—to Devonshire Street—past Old State House and Faneuil Hall—to Washington Street—through Dock Square—through Haymarket Square—to Washington Street North—over bridge to City Square, Charlestown—to Chelsea Street—to Wharfing Street—to Navy Yard—arriving there in time for the open air program to begin at 3 o'clock alongside "Old Ironsides".

MARSHAL—Captain Clarence A. Abele, U. S. N., commanding Massachusetts Nautical School Ship "Nantucket"; ADJUTANT— Capt. W. J. McCluskey, Marine Corps Reserves and staff.

FIRST DIVISION—Marshal and Staff—Crew of the U. S. S. Constitution— U. S. Coast Guard—U. S. Marine Reserves—U. S. Naval Reserves—Massachusetts Nautical School Cadets—Ancient and Honorable Artillery Company.

SECOND DIVISION—Veterans of the Grand Army of the Republic—Spanish War Veterans—American Legion Posts with Bands and Drum Corps—Veterans of Foreign Wars—Marine Corps League—Fleet Reserve Association with junior yachtsmen and drum corps—Naval Veterans Association of Lowell—Kearsarge Naval Veterans Association—Disabled American Veterans of the World War.

Patriotic and historical organizations—Sons of the American Revolution—Survivors of the Samoa Disaster—Society of War of 1812—Naval Order of the United States.

THIRD DIVISION—Boston School Cadets and Bands—Church boys organizations—Sea Scouts—Girl Scouts—Boy Scouts.

FOURTH DIVISION—Federal, State and Municipal officials, and the Committee of Arrangements, in automobiles.

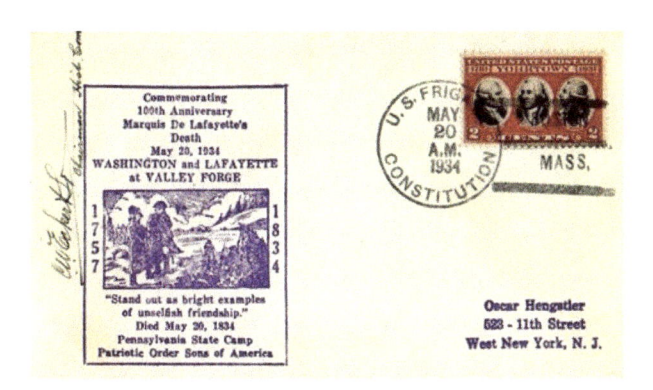

Cachet sponsor Pennsylvania State Camp, Patriotic Order Sons of America
First Appearance May 20

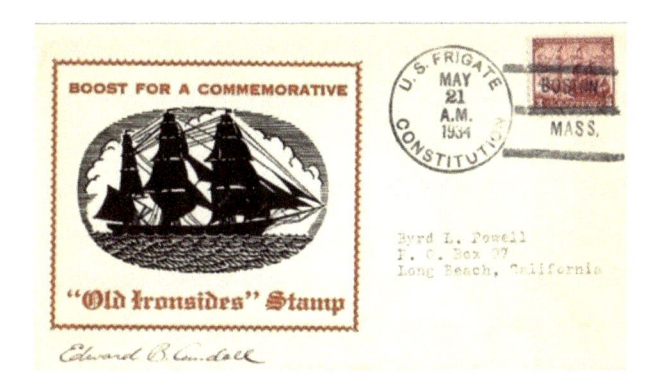

Cachet sponsor unknown
First Appearance May 21

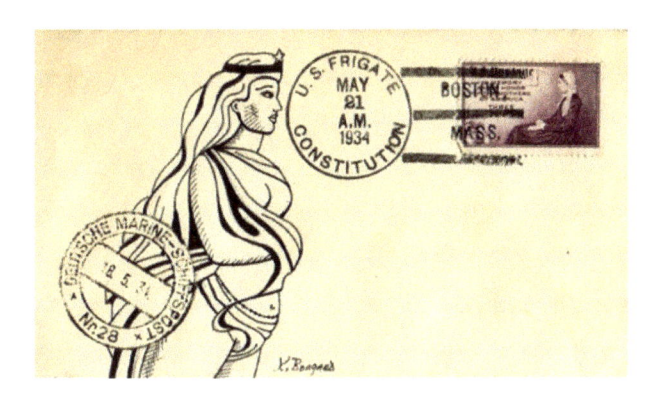

Cachet sponsor unknown
First Appearance May 21

PRIVATE: Cachet sponsor Oscar Hengstler
First Appearance May 16

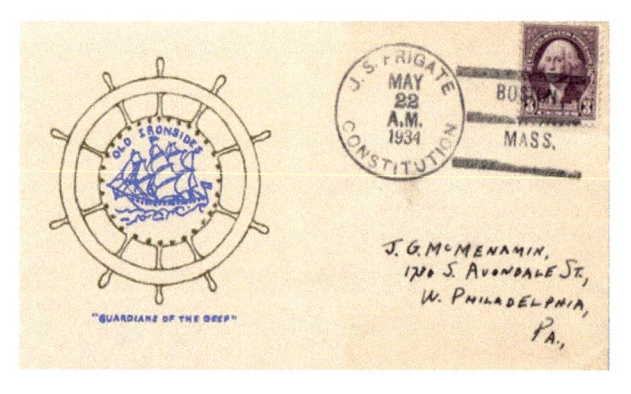

PRIVATE: Cachet sponsor unknown
First Appearance May 19

PRIVATE: Cachet sponsor unknown
First Appearance May 20

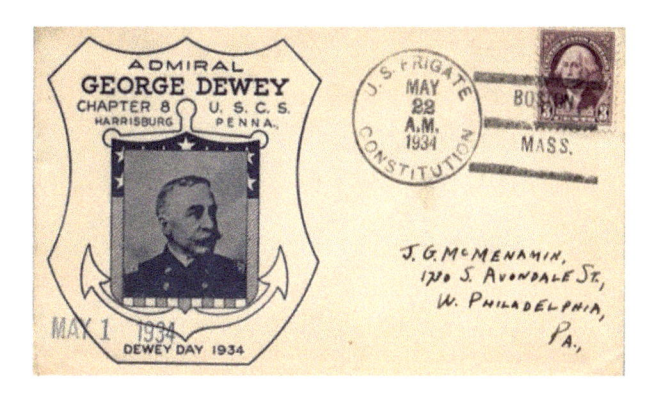

PRIVATE: Cachet sponsor Admiral George Dewey Chapter No. 8, USCS
First Appearance May 22

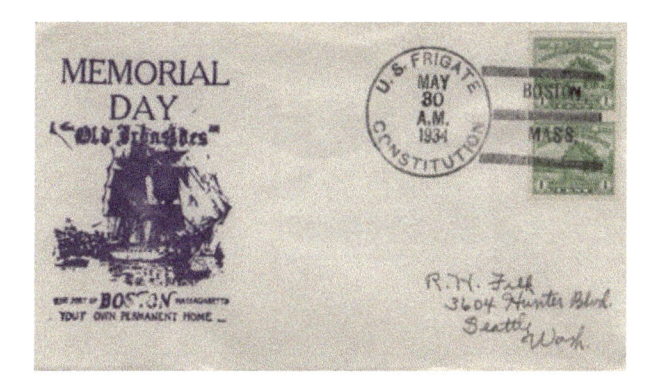

OFFICIAL: Cachet sponsor "Old Ironsides" Chapter No. 1 USCS
First Appearance May 30 (272 covers)

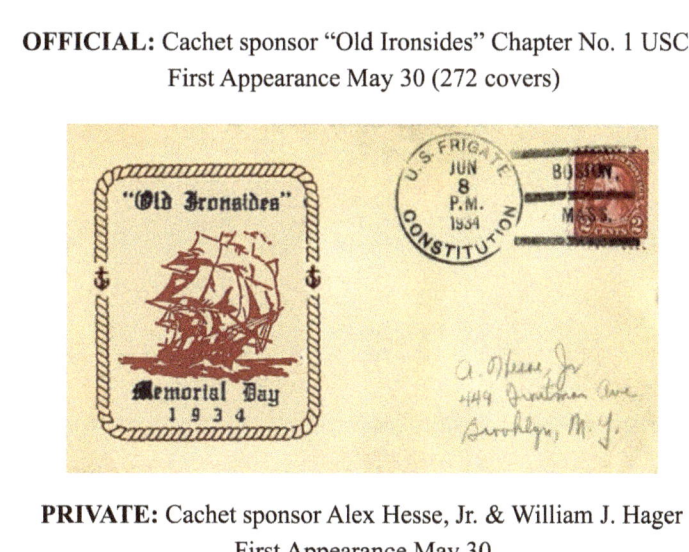

PRIVATE: Cachet sponsor Alex Hesse, Jr. & William J. Hager
First Appearance May 30

PRIVATE: Cachet sponsor John E. Gill
First Appearance May 30

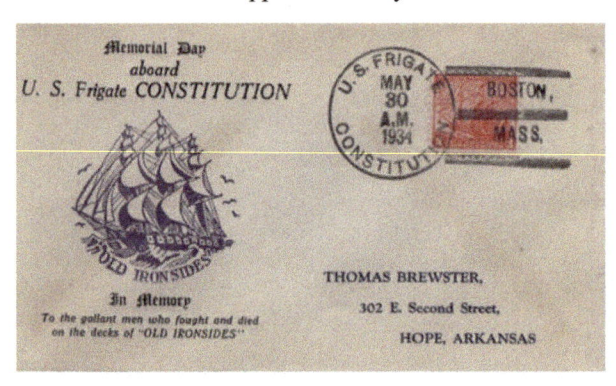

PRIVATE: Cachet sponsor Leonard Gilman
First Appearance May 30 (75 covers)

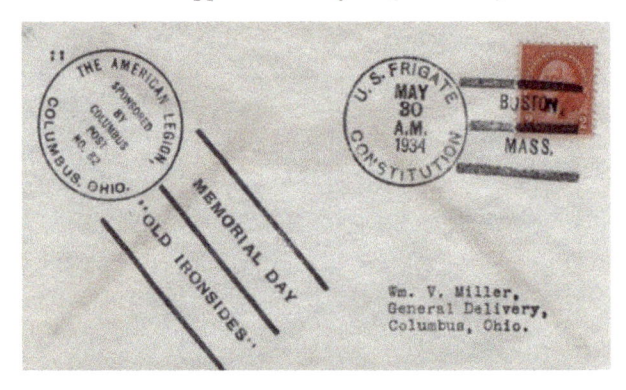

PRIVATE: Cachet sponsor American Legion Columbus Post No. 82
First Appearance May 30

PRIVATE: Cachet sponsor Oscar Hengstler
First Appearance May 30

PRIVATE: Cachet sponsor William V. Miller
First Appearance May 30

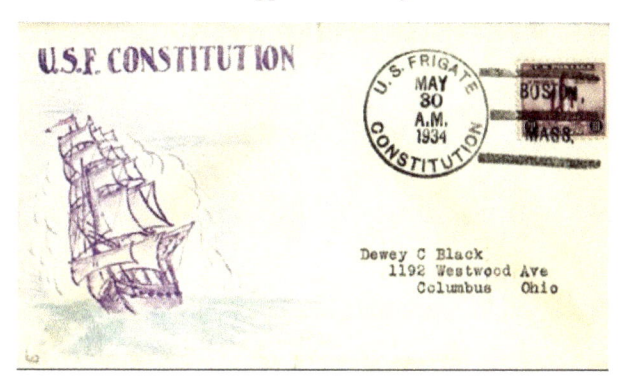

PRIVATE: Cachet sponsor Donald A. Schramm & C. Wright Richell
First Appearance May 30

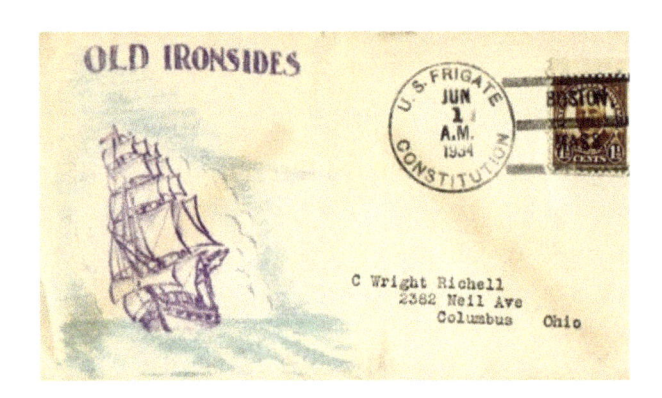

PRIVATE: Cachet sponsor Donald A. Schramm & C. Wright Richell
First Appearance June 1

Greeting *Constitution* on return to Boston - May 7, 1934

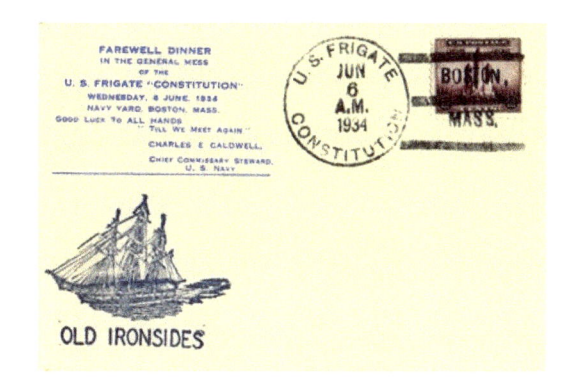

PRIVATE: Cachet sponsor Charles E. Caldwell
First Appearance June 6 - (Blue with S6 in Blue)

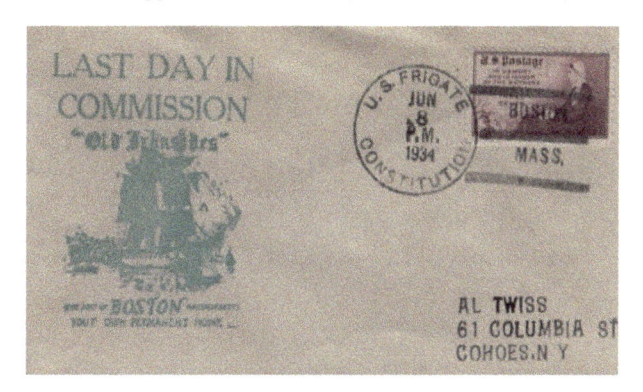

OFFICIAL: Cachet sponsor "Old Ironsides" Chapter No. 1 USCS
First Appearance June 8 (958 covers)

OFFICIAL: Cachet sponsor John E. Gill
First Appearance June 8

PRIVATE: Cachet sponsor Boston Cachet Cover Committee
First Appearance June 8

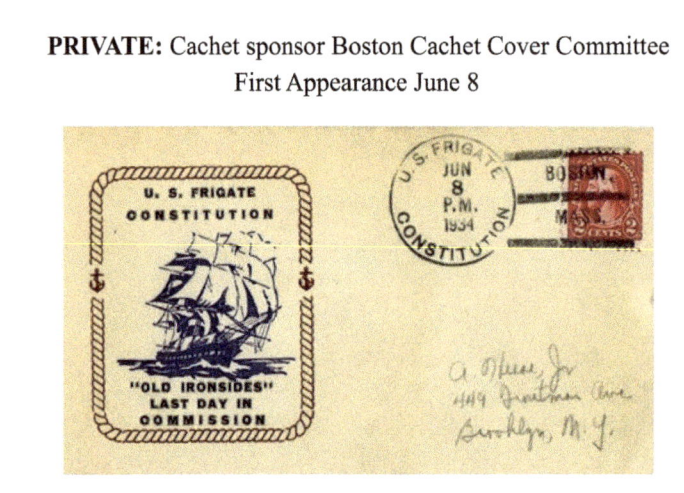

PRIVATE: Cachet sponsor Alex Hesse Jr & William J. Hager
First Appearance June 8

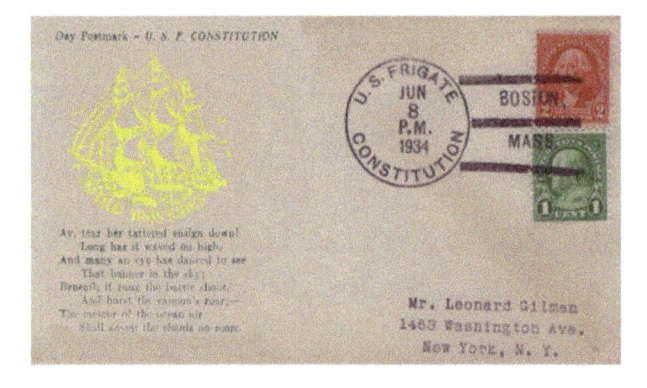

PRIVATE: Cachet sponsor Leonard Gilman
First Appearance June 8 (130 covers)

PRIVATE: Cachet sponsor Leonard Gilman
First Appearance June 8

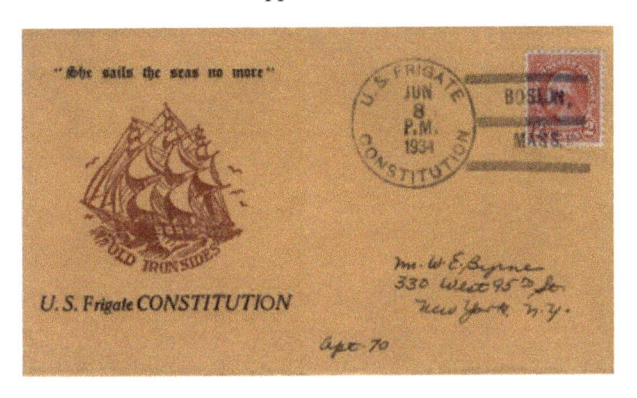

PRIVATE: Cachet sponsor Leonard Gilman
First Appearance June 8 (20 covers)

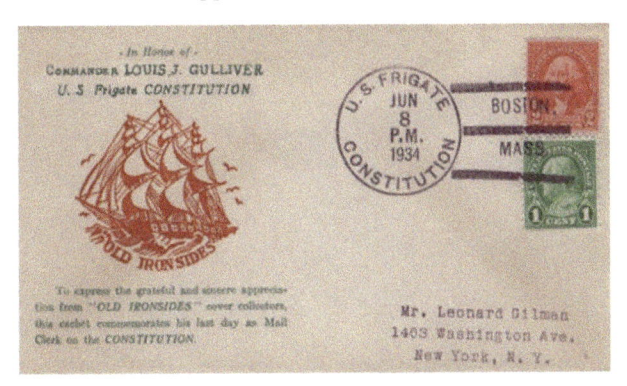

PRIVATE: Cachet sponsor Leonard Gilman
First Appearance June 8 (80 covers)

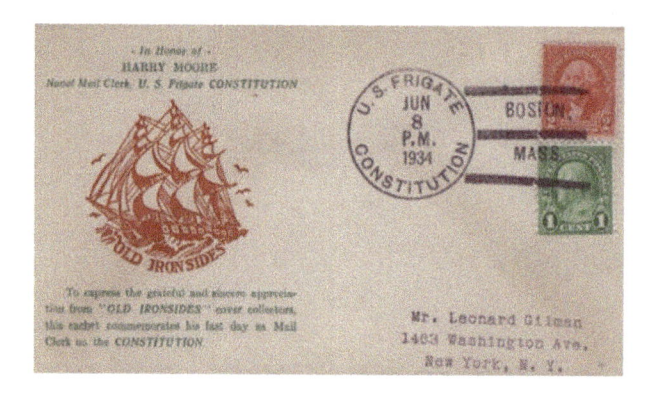

PRIVATE: Cachet sponsor Leonard Gilman
First Appearance June 8 (90 covers)

PRIVATE: Cachet sponsor Talbert A. Holland
First Appearance June 8

PRIVATE: Cachet sponsor Donald A. Schramm & C. Wright Richell
First Appearance June 8

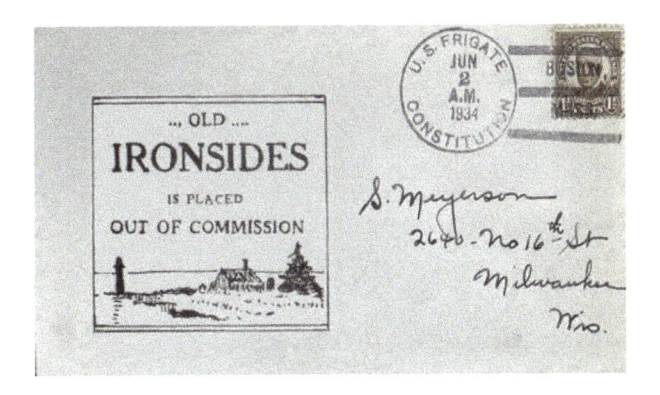

PRIVATE: Cachet sponsor Julius W. Hulff
First Appearance June 8 (25 covers)

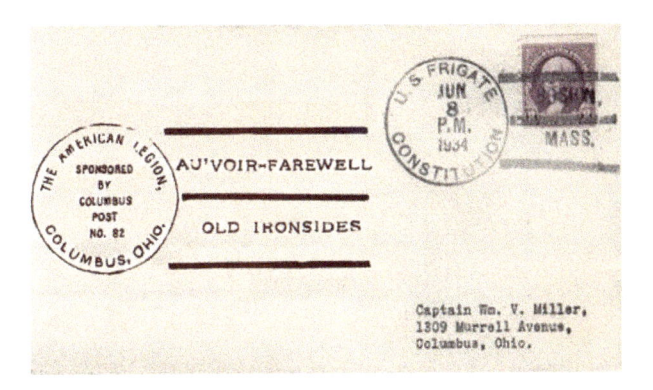

PRIVATE: Cachet sponsor William V. Miller
First Appearance June 8

PRIVATE: Cachet sponsor William V. Miller
First Appearance June 8

PRIVATE: Cachet sponsor Frank I Morse
First Appearance June 8

PRIVATE: Cachet sponsor Frank I. Morse
First Appearance June 8

PRIVATE: Cachet sponsor Oscar Hengstler
First Appearance June 8

PRIVATE: Cachet sponsor United States Daughters of 1812 Frigate Constitution Chapter
First Appearance June 8 (1104 covers)

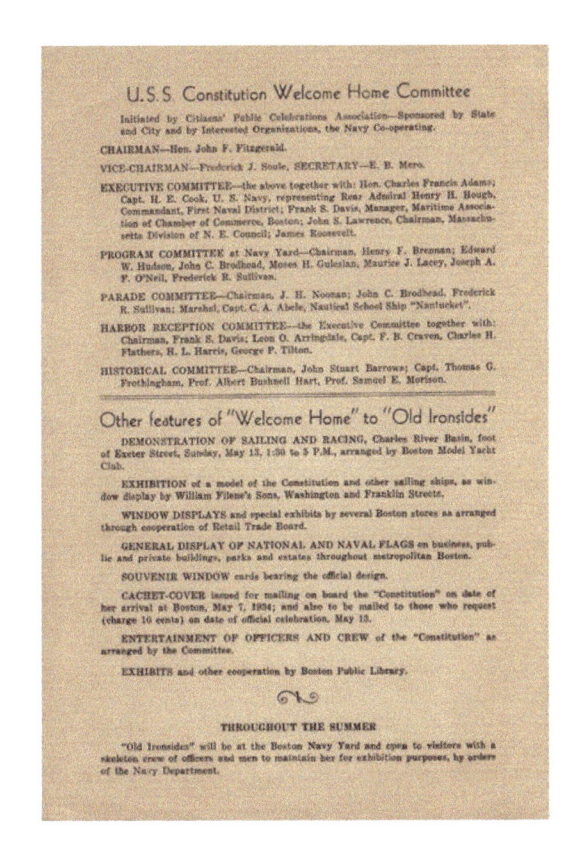

Appendix

USS *Constitution* Ports of Call - East/West Cruise
July 1, 1931 - June 8, 1934

Port of Call	Date Arrived	Date Departed	No. Visitors
Boston, MA		2-Jul-31	3,550
Gloucester, MA	2-Jul-31	3-Jul-31	0
Portsmouth, NH	3-Jul-31	12-Jul-31	31,102
Bar Harbor, ME	13-Jul-31	13-Jul-31	2,066
Bath, ME	14-Jul-31	1 7-Jul-31	11,904
Portland, ME	17-Jul-31	23-Jul-31	61,904
Gloucester, MA	23-Jul-31	29-Jul-31	19,603
Marblehead, MA	29-Jul-31	30-Jul-31	7,819
New Bedford, MA	31-Jul-31	6-Aug-31	58,710
Providence, RI	6-Aug-31	10-Aug-31	40,642
Newport, RI	10-Aug-31	13-Aug-31	8,962
New London, CT	13-Aug,31	20-Aug-31	36,211
Fort Pond Bay, NY	20-Aug-31	25-Aug-31	6,327
Oyster Bay, NY	25-Aug-31	28-Aug-31	4,061
New York, NY	29-Aug-31	14-Sep-31	102,307
Wilmington, DE	16-Sep-31	18-Sep-31	25,813
Philadelphia, PA	18-sep,31	1-Oct-31	154,803
Newport News, VA	2-Oct-31	9-Oct-31	34,512
Norfolk, VA	9-Oct-31	16-oct-31	85,950
Yorktown, VA	16-Oct,31	23-oct-31	17,788
Baltimore, MD	24-Oct,31	2-Nov,31	96,172
Annapolis, MD	2-Nov-31	5-Nov-31	7,988
Washington, D,C,	7-Nov-31	18-Nov-31	35,591
Wilmington, NC	21-Nov-31	30-Nov-31	46,716

City	Start	End	Amount
Charleston, SC	1-Dec-31	6-Dec-31	30,018
Savannah GA	7-Dec-31	11-Dec-31	33,848
Brunswick, GA	12-Dec-31	15-Dec-31	27,019
Jacksonville, FL	16-Dec-31	21-Dec-31	49,834
Miami, FL	23-Dec-31	30-Dec-31	48,924
Key west, FL	31-Dec-31	4-Jan-32	12,272
Pensacola, FL	6-Jan-32	11-Jan-32	36,051
Mobile, AL	11-Jan-32	18-Jan,32	119,704
Baton Rouge, LA	20-Jan-32	27-Jan-32	36,758
New Orleans, LA	27-Jan-32	13-Feb-32	193,431
Corpus Christi, TX	14-Feb-32	23-Feb-32	94,911
Galveston, TX	24-Feb-32	25-Feb-32	5
Houston, TX	25-Feb-32	1-Mar-32	110,406
Galveston, TX	1-Mar-32	7-Mar-32	39,783
Beaumont, TX	8-Mar-32	12-Mar-32	47,118
Port Arthur, TX	12-Mar-32	17-Mar-32	28,880
Orange, TX	17-Mar-32	19-Mar-32	11,337
Lake Charles, LA	19-Mar-32	22-Mar-32	37,657
Gulfport, MS	25-Mar-32	29-Mar-32	36,813
Port St, Joe, FL	30-Mar-32	1-Apr-32	7,479
Tampa, FL	3-Apr-32	7-Apr-32	63,056
St, Petersburg, FL	7-Apr-32	9-Apr-32	20,868
Quantico, VA	15-Apr-32	16-Apr-32	0
Washington, DC	16-Apr-32	11-May-32	10,984
Alexandria, VA	11-May-32	12-May-32	1,180
Washington, D,C,	12-May-32	8-Dec-32	118,327
Guantanamo Bay, Cuba	14-Dec-32	19-Dec-32	453
Cristobal, Panama	22-Dec-32	27-Dec-32	4,640
Balboa, Panama	27-Dec-32	7-Jan-33	11,110

San Diego, CA	21-Jan-33	16-Feb-33	178,599
San Pedro, CA	17-Feb-33	10-Mar-33	47,129
Long Beach, CA	10-Mar-33	19-Mar-33	85,426
Santa Barbara, CA	20-Mar-33	20-Mar-33	500
San Francisco, CA	24-Mar-33	12-Apr,33	311,379
Oakland, CA	12-Apr-33	26-Apr-33	200,247
Vallejo, CA	26-Apr-33	2-May-33	49,101
Astoria, OR	6-May-33	15-May-33	34,501
Gray's Harbor, WA	16-May-33	26-May-33	61,510
Port Angeles, WA	27-May-33	31-May-33	21,670
Seattle, WA	31-May-33	15-Jun-33	200,422
Tacoma, WA	15-Jun-33	22-Jun-33	84,595
Olympia, WA	22-Jun-33	1-Jul-33	35,886
Bremerton, WA	1-Jul-33	7-Jul-33	28,092
Everett, WA	7-Jul-33	14-Jul-33	55,797
Bellingham, WA	15-Jul-33	19-Jul-33	43,064
Anacortes, WA	20-Jul-33	26-Jul-33	27,699
Port Townsend, WA	26-Jul-33	30-Jul-33	5,898
Astoria, OR	31-Jul-33	2-Aug-33	0
Portland, OR	2-Aug-33	22-Aug-33	206,821
Kalama, WA	22-Aug-33	24-Aug-33	5,638
Longview, WA	24-Aug-33	26-Aug-33	23,597
San Francisco, CA	31-Aug-33	15-sep-33	42,372
Oakland, CA	15-Sept-33	29-Sep-33	27,335
Santa Cruz, CA	29-Sep-33	30-sep-33	905
Monterey, CA	30-Sep-33	1-Oct-33	1,657
Santa Barbara, CA	3-Oct-33	4-Oct-33	3,919
Ventura, CA	4-Oct-33	5-Oct-33	4,198
Santa Monica, CA	5-Oct-33	5-Oct-33	1,374

Long Beach, CA	6-Oct-33	19-Oct-33	67,892
San Pedro, CA	19-Oct-33	2-Nov-33	40,511
Avalon, CA	2-Nov-33	2-Nov-33	1,357
San Diego, CA	3-Nov-33	20-Mar-34	123,774
Balboa, Panama	2-Apr-34	7-Apr-34	2,404
Cristobal, Panama	7-Apr-34	3-May-34	0
St, Petersburg, FL	14-Apr-34	23-Apr-34	15,545
Charleston, SC	27-Apr-34	3-May-34	4,593
Boston, MA	7-May-34		31,741

Total Number of Stops **90** *Total number of Visitors* **4,210,715**

Checklist of Dates on which mail was canceled

1931

Boston, MA	July 1, 2
Gloucester, MA	July 3
Portsmouth, NH	July 4, 6
Bar Harbor, ME	July 13, 14
Bath, ME	July 15
Portland, ME	July 18
Gloucester, MA	July 29
Marblehead, MA	July 30
New Bedford, MA	July 31
Providence, RI	August 7, 8, 9, 10
Newport, RI	August 10, 11, 12, 13
New London, CT	August 14, 15, 16, 17, 18
Montauk, NY	August 21, 22
Oyster Bay, NY	August 25, 26
New York, New York	August 29, September 10, 14
Wilmington, DE	September 16, 17, 18
Philadelphia, PA	September 18, 19, 22-26, 28, 29, 30, October 1
Newport News, VA	October 2, 3, 5-9
Norfolk, VA	October 9, 10, 12-16
Yorktown, VA	October 16, 17, 18, 19, 21, 22, 23
Baltimore, MD	October 24-31, November 2
Annapolis, MD	November 2, 3, 4, 5
Quantico, VA	November 7
Washington, DC	November 7-18
Wilmington, NC	November 21-30
Charleston, SC	December 1, 2, 3, 4, 5, 6, 7
Savannah, GA	December 7, 8, 9, 10, 11
Brunswick, GA	December 12, 13, 14, 15
Jacksonville, FL	December 16, 17, 18, 19, 20, 21
Miami, FL	December 23, 24, 25, 28, 29, 30
Key West, FL	December 31

1932

Key West, FL	January 1, 2, 4
Pensacola, FL	January 6, 7, 8, 9, 10, 11
Mobile, AL	January 11-18
Baton Rouge, LA	January 20-26
New Orleans, LA	January 27-30, February 1-12
Enroute to Corpus Christi, TX	February 12
Corpus Christi, TX	February 14-23
Houston, TX	February 25-29, March 1
Galveston, TX	February 24, March 1, 2, 3, 4, 5, 6, 7
Beaumont, TX	March 8, 9, 10, 11, 12
Port Arthur, TX	March 12, 13, 14, 15, 16
Orange, TX	March 17, 18
Lake Charles, LA	March 19, 20, 21, 22
Gulfport, MS	March 25, 26, 27, 28, 29
Port Saint Joe, FL	March 30, 31, April 1
Tampa, FL	April 3, 4, 5, 6, 7
St. Petersburg, FL	April 7, 8, 9
Washington, DC	April 16-30, May 2-9
Alexandria, VA	May 11, 12
Washington, DC	All dates May 13 through December 8
Quantanamo Bay, Cuba	December 14, 15, 16, 17, 18, 19
Cristobal, Canal Zone	December 22, 23, 25, 27
Balboa, Canal Zone	December 27-31

1933

Balboa, Canal Zone	January 1, 4, 5, 6, 7
Latitude-Longitude	January 10, 12, 13, 14, 15, 18
San Diego, CA	January 21, 25-30, February 1-16
San Pedro, CA	February 17-28, March 1-10
Long Beach, CA	March 10-19
Santa Barbara, CA	March 24
San Francisco, CA	March 24-31, April 1-12
Oakland, CA	April 12-26
Vallejo, CA	April 26-30, May 2
Latitude-Longitude	May 4
Astoria, OR	May 6-15
Grays Harbor, WA	May 16-26
Port Angeles, WA	May 27, 28, 29, 30, 31
Seattle, WA	May 31, June 1-15
Tacoma, WA	June 15-22
Olympia, WA	June 22-30, July 1
Bremerton, WA	July 1, 2, 3, 4, 5, 6, 7
Edmonds, WA	July 7
Everett, WA	July 7-14
Bellingham, WA	July 14-20
Anacortes, WA	July 20, 21, 22, 23, 24, 25, 26
Port Townsend, WA	July 26, 27, 28, 29, 30
Latitude-Longitude	July 31
Tongue Point, OR	July 31, August 1, 2
Portland, OR	August 2-19, 22
Kalama, WA	August 22, 23, 24
Longview, WA	August 24, 25, 26, 27, 28
Off Oregon Coast	August 29
San Francisco, CA	August 31, September 2-15
Oakland, CA	September 15-29
Santa Cruz, CA	September 30
Monterey, CA	October 1
Port San Luis, CA	October 2
Santa Barbara, CA	October 3
Ventura, CA	October 4
Santa Monica, CA	October 5
Long Beach, CA	October 6-19
San Pedro, CA	October 19-31, November 1, 2
Avalon, CA	November 2
San Diego, CA	November 3-30, December 1-31

1934

San Diego, CA	January 1, 5-31, February 1-28, March 1-20
San Diego Harbor, CA	March 20
Enroute To Balboa, Canal Zone	March 22, 23
Latitude-Longitude	March 26
At Sea	March 26, 27
Gulf of Tehuantepec	March 27
Off Coast of Panama	April 1
Balboa, Canal Zone	April 2, 3, 4, 5, 6, 7
Transit RED Locks	April 7
Transit of Panama Canal	April 7
Cristobal, Canal Zone	April 7, 8
Latitude-Longitude	April 10
St. Petersburg, FL	April 14-23
Charleston, SC	April 27-30, May 1, 2, 3
Off Cape Hatteras	May 4
Boston, MA	May 7-31, June 1, 2, 3, 4, 5, 6, 7, 8

Harry Moore "Log" Covers

During the *Constitution*'s East/West Cruise (1931 – 1934), Harry Moore, the mail clerk, produced a number of special covers. These covers had the appropriate *Constitution* postmark for the particular port with the arrival or departure date/time typed in the upper left corner of the cover. Below the date/time, was two sections of 3 – 4 typed lines of either a fact of the port, or of the *Constitution*. Harry Moore produced a handful of the covers as an unofficial "log" of the *Constitution*'s cruise. Probably due to the immense number of covers presented for postmark on the *Constitution*, Harry Moore only made these covers for the East coast portion of the cruise. Following is a selection of those covers the author was able to locate. It must be noted here that although there are covers for Providence, RI and Newport, RI, these covers were produced at a date later than what is on the covers.

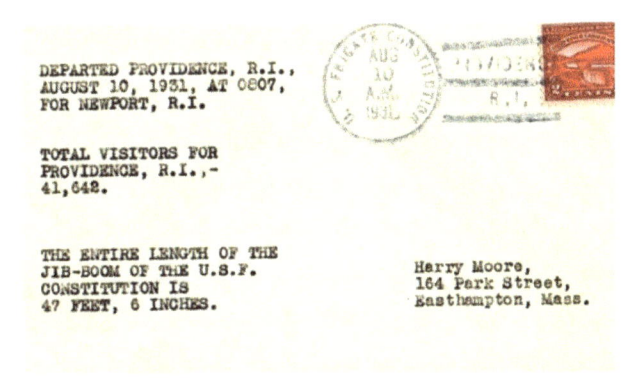

Departed Providence, RI – August 10, 1931

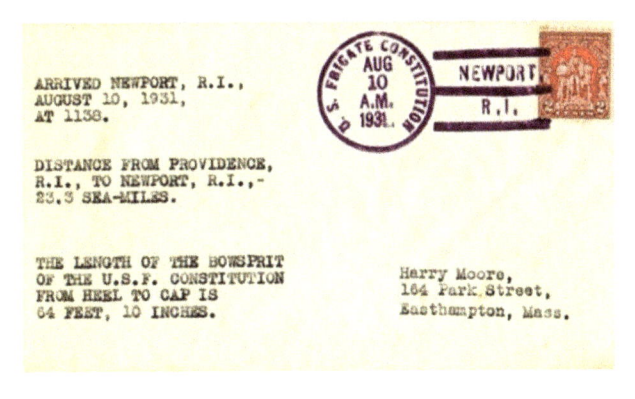

Arrival Newport, RI – August 10, 1931

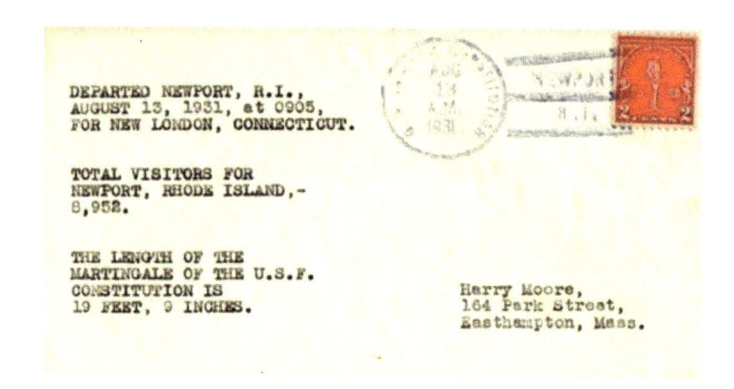

Departed Newport, RI – August 13, 1931

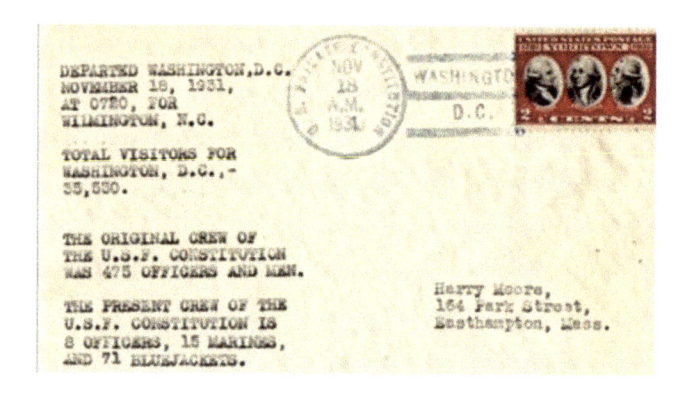

Departed Washington, DC - November 18, 1931

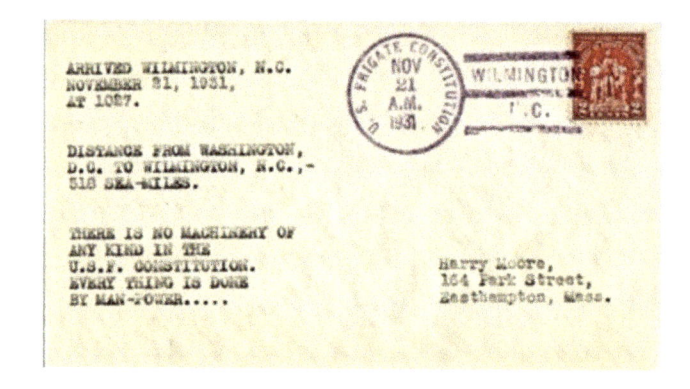

Arrived Wilmington, NC - November 21, 1931

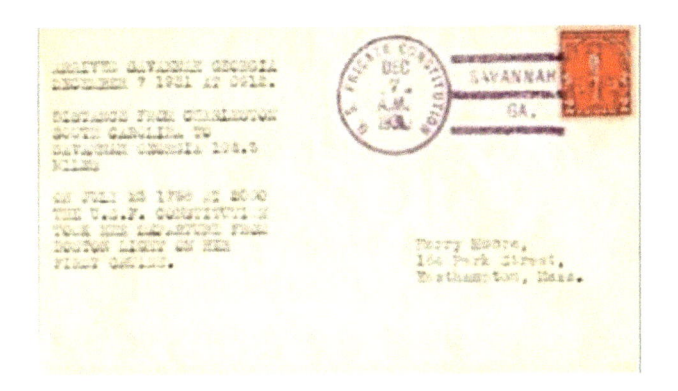

Arrived Savannah, GA - December 7, 1931

Arrived Jacksonville, FL - December 16, 1931

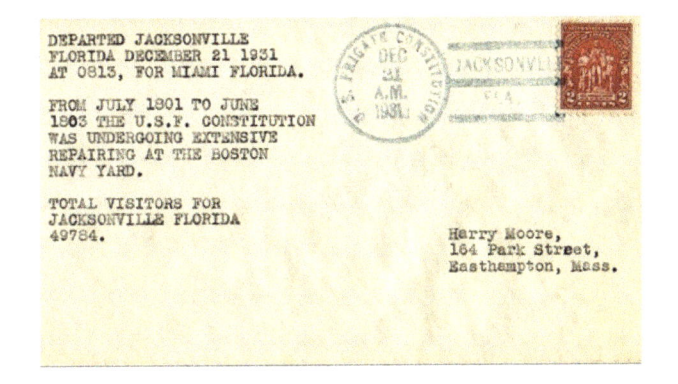

Departed Jacksonville, FL - December 21, 1931

Arrived Miami, FL - December 23, 1931

Departed Miami, FL - December 31, 1931

Arrived Key West, FL - December 31, 1931

Departed Key West, FL - January 4, 1932

Set of "Boost Old Ironsides" stamps created by W. G. Crosby
Seen on many covers of USS *Constitution* in 1934
(Individual stamps shown below)

Autographs

Following is a sample of autographs of those responsible for making the selection of cachet envelopes possible on the USS *Constitution's* East/West Cruise of 1931 – 1934. While there are possibly many more available, these are here for your enjoyment.

For the *Constitution*

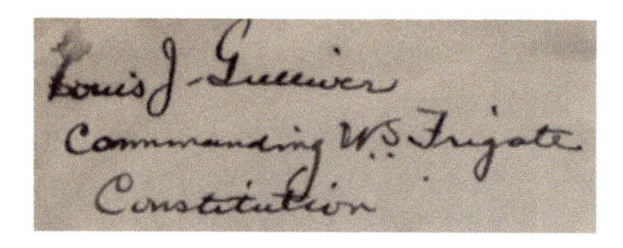

Louis J. Gulliver
Commander

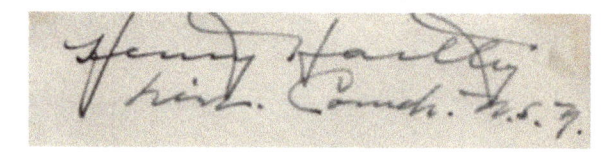

Henry Hartley
Executive Officer

Harry Moore
Mail Clerk

F. A. Majerowski
Temporary replacement when Moore was injured
Served Nov. 2, 1933 - Nov. 14, 1933 (approx.)

For the Sponsors, Designers, and Directors

Louis T. Moore
Cachet Director, Wilmington, NC – November 1931

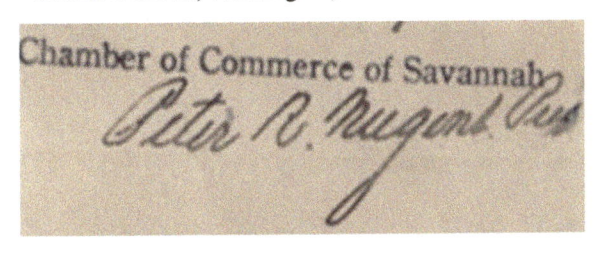

Peter Nugent
Cachet Sponsor. Savannah, GA – November 1931

Raleigh D. Newton
Cachet Designer, San Pedro, CA - February 1933

Emil A. Thurman
Cachet Director, New Orleans, LA - February 1932

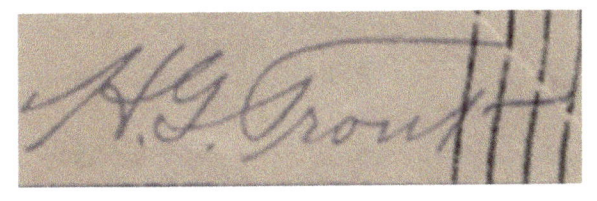

H. G. Trout
Cachet Director, Long Beach, CA – March 1933

Roy Sherman
Cachet Director, Vallejo, CA – April 1933

Cachet Director, Seattle, WA – May 1933

L. M Ryder
Cachet Designer, Seattle, WA - May 1933

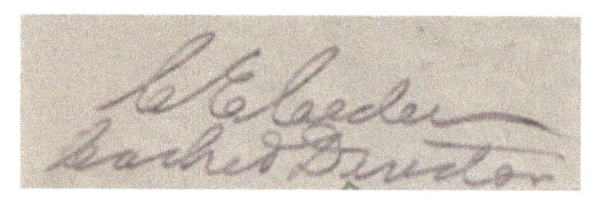

C. Edward Ceder
Cachet Director, Tacoma, WA – June 1933

Lt. A. D. Hunter, U.S.N.
Cachet Director & Designer, Bremerton, WA – July 1933

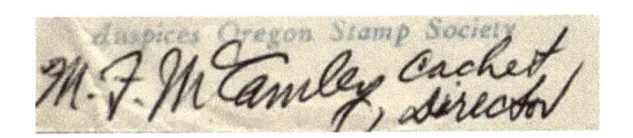

Myron F. McCamley
Cachet Designer & Director, Portland, OR – August 1933

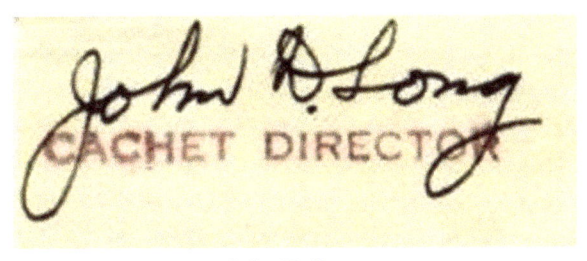

John D. Long
Cachet Director, San Francisco, CA – August 1933

Clyde Welsh
Cachet Designer & Director, Oakland CA – September 1933

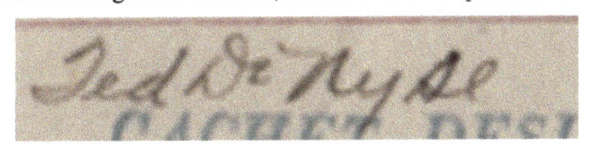

Ted De Nyse
Cachet Designer, Long Beach, CA – October 1933

Byrd L. Powell
Cachet Director, Long Beach, CA – October 1933

W. G. Crosby
Cachet Director, Long Beach, CA – October 1933

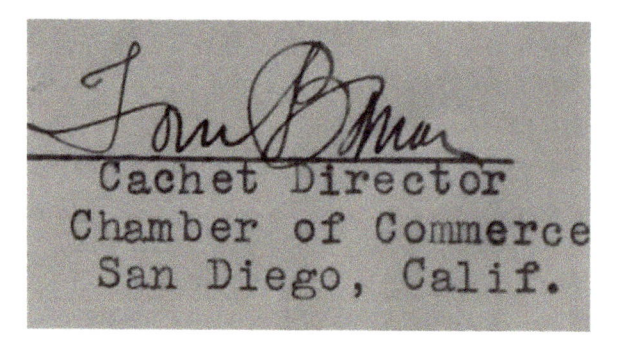

Thomas Bomar
Cachet Director, San Diego, CA – November 1933

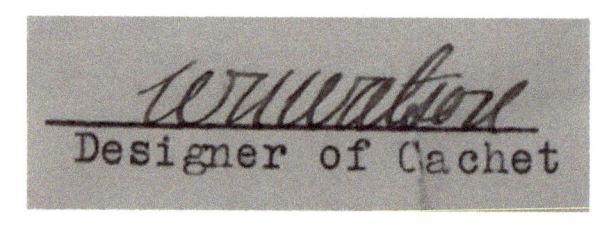

Willard N. Watson
Cachet Designer, San Diego, CA – November 1933

C. G. Morris
Cachet Designer, San Diego, CA – February 1934

David Brockton Browne
Cachet Sponsor, San Diego, CA – January 1934

Edward E. Bryan
Cachet Sponsor, San Diego, CA – March 1934

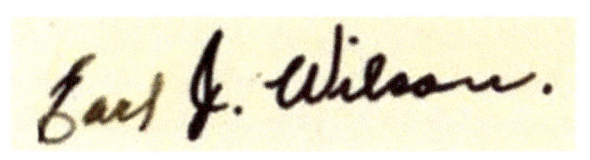

Earl J. Wilson
Cachet Sponsor, St. Petersburg, FL – April 1934

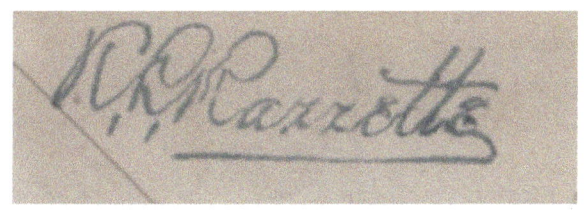

R. L. Razzette
Cachet Sponsor, Charleston, SC – April 1934

E. E. Ward, Jr.
Cachet Sponsor, Charleston, SC – April 1934

Frank I. Morse
Cachet Sponsor, Boston, MA – May 1934

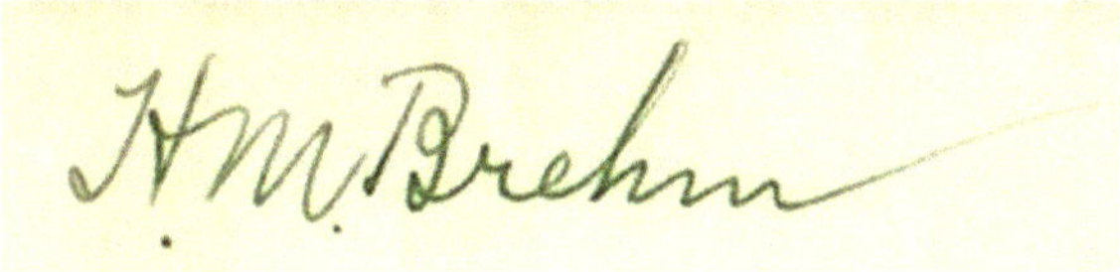

H. M. Brehm
Cachet Sponsor, San Diego - February 1933

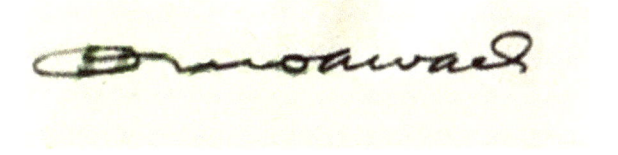

A. Moawad
Cachet Sponsor, Kalama, WA - August 1933

Donald A. Schramm
Cachet Sponsor, San Diego, CA - February 1934

Frank I. Morse
Cachet Sponsor, Boston, MA – May 1934

Joseph Webster
Apprentice Boy, USS *Constitution* - 1881
Seattle - June 1933

USS *Constitution* Crew List 1931 – 1934 Cruise

Following is a list of Officers (7), Enlisted Naval Crew (65), and Marines (15) who served on-board the *Constitution during the cruise.*

Officers

Gulliver, Louis J., Commander, Captain of *Constitution*
Hartley, Henry, Lieutenant Commander, Executive Officer of *Constitution*
Dannenberg, J. Y., Lieutenant
Dean, W. J., Lieutenant
Lyon, D. W., Lieutenant, Medical Officer
Tolson, David W., Lieutenant
Van Cleve, Joseph C., Lieutenant

Crew

Achers, C.	Flores, J.
Babishkewich, A. J.	Flynn, J. M.
Beckman, E.	Galaske, Henry
Beland, Joseph Severe Emile	Gauvain, J. A. R.
Bellavance, J. A.	Glass, Jesse Hamilton
Berger, G. C.	Goodson, J. W.
Blanchard, Benjamin E.	Griffith, J. H.
Breau, J. A.	Hosford, R. M.
Bystizcycki, Sigmund	Howe, C. C.
Caldeney, H. E.	Howe, G. B.
Caldwell, C. E.	Indigaro, E. D.
Cantwell, C. P.	Johansen, E. M.
Church, J. A.	Johnson, T. I.
Colson, V. M.	Jones, H. E.
Conroy, T. J.	Jordan, R. G.
Crow, R.	King, G. C.
Damizio, Martin	Kisela, J.
Dauphinais, J.	Kivinsky, J.
De La Cruz, A.	Kivinsky, J.
Dougherty, T. P.	Kraul, J. B.
Dunham, A. C	Littlejohn, J.
Duponti, N.	Lyons, E. J.
Dyer, J. T.	Lyons, W. J.
Elliott, F. P.	Majerowski, F. A.
Evens, P. R.	Marzan, T.
Febig, O. G.	Matthews, R. W.

Metross, G. P.
Mojica, G.
Moore, Harry A.
Morin, Joseph
Movido, L.
Ona, M.
Palermo, J.
Parish, G. W.
Perez, C.
Pruaz, Franciezek "Frank"
Purcer, N. H.
Purganan, G.
Pyle, M. R.
Quandt, R. W.
Ramirez, T.

Savell, C. K.
Schilling, A. J.
Schmidt, J. F.
Sheets, J. K.
Shiflet, Roy
Stow, E. M.
Therrien, R. J.
Towery, H. M.
Tytler, James William
Wallace, C.
Webb, R.
Wentworth, E. E.
Whitmire, G. R.
Young, P.

US Navy General Order No. 74 of 27 June 1908
Establishing Ship Post Offices

GENERAL ORDER   NAVY DEPARTMENT
No. 74   WASHINGTON, June 27, 1908

1. The following act of Congress, approved May 27, 1908, is published for the information and guidance of the naval service:

> That enlisted men of the United States Navy may, upon selection by the Secretary of the Navy, be designated by the Post Office Department as "navy mail clerks" and "assistant navy mail clerks," who shall be authorized to receive and open all pouches and sacks of mail, to receive matter for transmission in the mails, to receipt for registered matter (keeping an accurate record thereof), to keep and have for sale an adequate supply of postage stamps, to make up and dispatch mails, and other postal duties as may be authorized by the Postmaster-General, all in accordance with such rules and regulations as may be prescribed by the commanding officer of the vessel or of the squadron to which the vessel is attached. Each mail clerk and assistant mail clerk shall take the oath of office prescribed for employees of the postal service and shall give bond to the United States in the sum of one thousand dollars for the faithful performance of his duties as such clerk, and shall be amenable in all respect to naval discipline, except that, as to their duties as such clerks, the commanding officers of the vessels upon which they are stationed shall require them to be governed by the postal laws and regulations of the United States.

Whenever necessity arises therefor any assistant mail clerk may be required by the commanding officer of the vessel upon which he is stationed or of the squadron to which said vessel is attached to perform the duties of mail clerk. They shall receive as compensation for such services form the Navy Department, in addition to that paid them of the grade to which they are assigned, such sum in the case of mail clerks not to exceed five hundred dollars per annum, and in that of assistant mail clerks not to exceed three hundred dollars per annum, as may be determined and allowed by the Navy Department.

2. In accordance with the above act, vessels of the United States Navy having a complement of 650 or more officers and men, and receiving ships, will be allowed a navy mail clerk and an assistant navy mail clerk; vessels having a complement of 125 or more, and less than 650, officers and men will be allowed a navy mail clerk; and in a regularly organized flotilla having a total complement of 125 or more officers and men the flagboat will be allowed a navy mail clerk.

3. Instructions and regulations governing navy mail clerks and assistant navy mail clerks and blank forms of bonds will be issued by the Post Office Department and transmitted through the Navy Department to commanders in chief, commanders of divisions, and commanding officers of vessels. Upon notification by the Post Office Department that he has been duly designated, each navy mail clerk and assistant navy mail clerk shall, as soon as practicable, sign a separate blank bond in the presence of two witnesses, who shall certify to the signature. The bond shall then be forwarded to a surety company for completion and transmission to the Department for approval by the Secretary of the Navy. Any company authorized under the act of August 13, 1894, to do business in United States matters will be acceptable to the Post Office Department as a surety on the bond in question.

4. Before entering upon their postal duties, navy mail clerks and assistant navy mail clerks shall take and subscribe before a magistrate or commissioned officer of the Navy and transmit to the Department the following oath, required by section 391 of the Revised Statues:

> I, A. B., do solemnly swear (or affirm) that I will faithfully perform all the duties required of me, and abstain from everything forbidden by the laws in relation to the establishment of post-offices, and post-roads within the United States; and that I will honestly and truly account for and pay over any money belonging to the said United States which may come into my possession or control. So help me, God.

5. Enlisted men of the Navy designated as navy mail clerks shall receive, in addition to the monthly pay of their rating, the following compensation for their services: On vessels having a complement of 650 or more officers and men, and on receiving ships, $25 per month; on vessels and in flotillas having a complement of 250 or more, and less than 650, officers and men, $20 per month; on vessels and in flotillas having a complement of 125 or more, and less than 250, officers and men, $15 per month. Enlisted men of the Navy designated as assistant mail clerks shall receive for their services $15 pr month in addition to the monthly pay of their rating.

6. The compensation of navy mail clerks and assistant navy mail clerks, for services as such, shall begin upon the date when they take the oath of office and enter upon postal duties and close on the date of the termination of such services, and shall be paid out of the appropriation, "Pay of the Navy." The commanding officer of the vessel, or of the fleet or division to which the vessel is attached, may direct the termination of such services at any time, reporting the fact to the Navy Department, which will inform the Post Office Department.

7. An assistant navy mail clerk shall assist the navy mail clerk in the performance of his duties as such clerk; and whenever the necessity arises therefor, an assistant navy mail clerk may be designated by the commanding officer of the vessel upon which he is stationed, or of the fleet or division to which the vessel is attached, to perform the duties of navy mail clerk. On board any ship that is not allowed a navy mail clerk, or on which a navy mail clerk is not detailed, or serving as such, the mails shall be handled in accordance with the Navy Regulations.

8. Commanding officers shall recommend to the Secretary of the Navy competent and desirable enlisted men of the Navy under their command to render service as navy mail clerks and assistant navy mail clerks, and the names of those selected will be submitted to the Post Office Department for designation. The Department shall be informed by letter of the date of the execution of the oath of office of each naval mail clerk and assistant navy mail clerk and of the date of termination of such service.

Published: Thu Jan 31 18:15:18 EST 2019 by Naval History and Heritage Command

USS *Constitution* returned to Boston